D0597541

DEMCO

99%
FAT-FREE
Meals in 30 Minutes

Also by Barry Bluestein and Kevin Morrissey

The 99% Fat-Free Cookbook

The 99% Fat-Free Book of Appetizers and Desserts

The Complete Cookie

Home Made in the Kitchen

The Bountiful Kitchen

Light Sauces

Quick Breads

Doubleday

NEW YORK LONDON
TORONTO SYDNEY AUCKLAND

99%
FAT-FREE
Meals in 30 Minutes

Scrumptious Menus for Complete Meals that

Can Be Made in About 30 Minutes—

with No More than 1 Gram of Fat per Dish

Barry Bluestein
& Kevin Morrissey

PUBLISHED BY DOUBLEDAY
a division of Bantam Doubleday Dell Publishing Group, Inc.
1540 Broadway, New York, New York 10036

DOUBLEDAY and the portrayal of an anchor with a dolphin are trademarks of
Doubleday, a division of Bantam Doubleday Dell Publishing Group, Inc.

Book design by Donna Sinisgalli

Library of Congress Cataloging-in-Publication Data
Bluestein, Barry.
99% fat-free meals in 30 minutes : scrumptious menus for complete meals that can
be made in about 30 minutes—with no more than 1 gram of fat per dish / Barry
Bluestein and Kevin Morrissey. — 1st ed.
p.   cm.
Includes index.
1. Quick and easy cookery.   2. Low-fat diet—Recipes.
I. Morrissey, Kevin.   II. Title.
TX833.5.B57   1998
641.5′638—dc21   97-13421
                                                    CIP

ISBN 0-385-48544-1
Copyright © 1998 by Barry Bluestein and Kevin Morrissey
All Rights Reserved
Printed in the United States of America
February 1998
First Edition
1 3 5 7 9 10 8 6 4 2

For Eleanor Bluestein,

just because . . .

Acknowledgments

First and foremost, thanks to our editor, Judy Kern, the best in the biz. And to so many others at Doubleday for their belief in us and our books, including Jackie Everly, Valerie Peterson, Tammy Blake, Skip Dye, Dorothy Auld, and Brandon Saltz. As always, to Carol Siegel for her careful copyedit, and to Susan Ramer, our literary agent, for her unstinting support.

For hands-on assistance with several menus, we acknowledge Ann Bloom-strand. For ideas, advice, and encouragement, Cheryl Blumenthal, Rosie Daley, Lisa Ekus, Merrilyn Lewis, Karen Peltier, Claudia Clark Potter, William Rice, Martha Scheuneman, Michael Silverstein, Mara Tapp, and Jill Van Cleave. And for cook-ware and bakeware that make our work a lot easier, Cheryl McDaniel and Mark Sterwald of the Mirro Company.

Contents

Introduction

Much like the most famous road in the history of human endeavor, the path to a more healthful American diet is paved with good intentions.

We no longer need to be educated about the perils of our traditionally high-fat diet. We fully comprehend the role that lowering fat intake can play in controlling numerous preventable, dietary-related health problems. We understand the important distinction between simply paring calories and reducing calories derived from fat. We get the big picture.

Yet the gap between understanding the need to adopt more healthful eating habits and actually doing so on a day-to-day basis is persistent and troublesome.

The origins of the problem appear to be twofold: Most of us don't seem to know how to alter our home-cooking methods systematically in ways that will consistently yield satisfying meals stripped of superfluous fat. And most of us tend to believe that preparing more healthful meals from scratch is just too time-consuming and complex a task to pursue on a daily basis.

We addressed the first problem in *The 99% Fat-Free Cookbook* and *The 99% Fat-Free Book of Appetizers and Desserts*, which introduced a comprehensive approach to low-fat cooking distinguished by its diner-friendly perspective.

By breaking down traditional recipes and rebuilding them in ways that pare significant amounts of fat at the source, that is, in the kitchen, the 99% fat-free method of cooking frees diners from regimented diets and enables healthful eating without

deprivation. It provides cooks with simple techniques to select ingredients judiciously, to prepare these ingredients innovatively, and to dispense with such ingrained habits as automatically reaching for a fat-laden bottle of oil when pursuing as basic a task as sautéing.

In this volume, we tackle the time factor. We set out to demonstrate not only that low-fat meals can be so flavorful and filling that you will want to eat more healthfully on a daily basis, but also that low-fat cooking can be sufficiently quick and easy to fit into even the busiest schedule.

99% Fat-Free Meals in 30 Minutes features dozens of menus—from elegant dinner party food to family meals to lunch, brunch, and casual dinner fare—that can be prepared in about 30 minutes, with no single dish containing more than 1 gram of fat. Bear in mind that some menus may take some cooks 40 minutes or more, others might be executed in well under 30 minutes. The "99% Fat-Free Fast Strategy" for each menu provides straightforward advice on integrating the recipe steps for each dish in the menu in the most timesaving fashion. Individual recipes in each menu are arranged in the order in which they first appear in the strategy.

Our "99% Fat-Free Fast Pantry" explains how to stock your cupboards, refrigerator, and freezer, taking full advantage of the selection of the pretrimmed, prechopped, precleaned, and precooked ingredients now proliferating on supermarket shelves. We include a chapter of virtually fat-free desserts—a mouth-watering selection from which you can choose a fitting finale for almost any type of meal.

Maintaining a healthy, low-fat diet need not deprive the diner nor hold the cook captive in the kitchen. Savor these satisfying, easily prepared meals with our slogan in mind: Minimal work, minimal time, minimal fat!

The 99%
Fat-Free
Fast Pantry

~

Counts, Measurements, and Equivalents

The total fat per serving has been calculated for each recipe to the nearest one hundredth of a gram, and total calories to the nearest one tenth of a calorie. For commercial ingredients, we use the lowest-fat brands readily available; always compare nutritional labels carefully.

For greater accuracy in calculating fat and calories, most raw ingredients are specified by weight. To help you shop, we generally provide equivalents for weight measurements unless the measured quantity is derived from less than a whole ingredient. For example:

8 ounces Italian plum tomatoes (about 2 tomatoes)

6 ounces yellow summer squash (also called crookneck squash; about 1 squash)

1 pound purple eggplant (about 1 small eggplant)

8 ounces red bell pepper (about 1 pepper)

Cup measurements are provided for ingredients subsequently chopped or diced.

Much supermarket produce is now available in handy precut form, saving precious time that would otherwise be spent trimming and cutting. We call for precut produce in the case of those ingredients readily available in this form. For example:

chopped white onion

sliced white button mushrooms

cut romaine lettuce leaves and other salad
    mixes

trimmed baby or salad spinach leaves

shredded and baby-cut carrots

shredded cabbage

broccoli florets

cauliflower florets

Ingredients

ASIAN NOODLES: The growing availability of Asian noodles, such as rice stick vermicelli, cellophane noodles, and fresh chow mein noodles, on supermarket shelves has done much to expand our repertoire of quick-to-prepare fat-free dishes. Most are made without flour or egg, which add superfluous fat, and they're very fast cooking. Using our recipes as a point of departure, we recommend creative experimentation with these products in your own fat-free kitchen.

ASIAN SAUCES: We make full use of the multitude of flavorful Asian sauces now on the market, including red chili paste, red curry paste, black bean garlic sauce, and chili paste with garlic, as well as hoisin, fish, oyster, and soy sauces. Many supermarkets now stock a surprising range of sauces in their ethnic section; if yours doesn't, try an Asian grocery.

BEANS: We call for a range of canned beans in our recipes for convenience, eliminating the added time and effort that would be required to soak and cook dried beans. Always rinse and drain canned beans before proceeding to use them in the recipe.

If you want to use dried beans and are willing to invest an extra 10 to 25 minutes at mealtime, set the beans aside to soak before you start your day and cook them in a pressure cooker according to the manufacturer's directions.

BISCUITS: See page 20.

BREAD CRUMBS: As all of the prepared bread crumbs we know of have a higher fat content than we budget for this ingredient, we make our own. One slice of bread yields 4 to 5 tablespoons of bread crumbs. Use French Bread (page 19) or a commercial product low in fat, such as some light oatmeal breads.

CHICKEN STOCK: See page 13.

COCOA POWDER: Recipes are based upon use of Dutch (or European style) processed cocoa powder, which produces a different chemical reaction than other cocoas that are not treated with an alkali.

COCONUT MILK: Until recently, the inherent fat content of coconut milk prohibited its use in fat-free cooking. There's now a light version that can be used in small quantities. Look in the Asian aisle of your supermarket.

CURRY POWDER: See page 22.

EGG SUBSTITUTE AND EGG WHITE: We use both nonfat liquid egg substitute (the variety that can be stored in the freezer and kept far longer than shell eggs) and egg whites. In many cases, they can be used interchangeably; 2 egg whites equal $\frac{1}{4}$ cup of egg substitute. The exceptions are the Carrot Soufflé (page 174), which requires egg whites, and the Potato and Pepper Frittata (page 57), which needs the color provided by the egg substitute. Read labels carefully and be sure to choose a nonfat product.

FINES HERBES: See page 21.

FLATBREAD: This product may also be labeled mountain bread, untoasted lavasch, or single pita. Select the thinnest and most pliable you can find for ease in assembling wraps and rolls, and be sure to avoid varieties made with oil.

FRENCH BREAD: See page 19.

FRUIT: Look for precut cantaloupe for the Spicy Shrimp and Melon Salad (page 107) in your market's produce section or on the salad bar, and for the grapefruit sections (in a jar) for the Citrus Salsa (page 151) in the produce refrigerator case.

We put old-fashioned canned fruit in heavy syrup to a thoroughly modern use in several dessert recipes. The sorbets included in our *99% Fat-Free Book of Appetizers and Desserts* proved to be quite popular, but preparation of similar recipes in an ice cream maker would take too long to fit within this volume's self-imposed time constraints. We've since learned that canned fruit in syrup, when frozen, could serve as the basis for delightful sorbets and sherbets that can be made in the food processor in minutes; freeze the fruit in the can for at least 8 hours. (See the Desserts chapter.)

GARLIC: In addition to the minced and chopped garlic sold in jars in supermarket produce aisles, which have long been a lifesaver to harried cooks, these days one can often find minced roasted garlic as well.

There's no last-minute peeling and chopping when you use precut garlic, and you never have to face the dilemma of whether to increase the volume called for or toss the inevitable half a clove extra that you've chopped. Alternatively, you can chop garlic ahead of time in a mini food processor, as we often do. Stored in a small, tight-sealing container, it will keep fresh for a week to ten days in the refrigerator.

GINGER: Many better produce departments now stock grated ginger in jars, which can save you not only time, but also considerable wear and tear on your knuckles.

In some recipes, we use fresh ginger juice, derived simply by wrapping the specified quantity of grated ginger tightly in paper toweling and squeezing the juice into the pot or bowl.

GNOCCHI: See page 17.

HERBS AND SPICES: We use fresh herbs from the supermarket in volume, sub-stituting dried herbs for quickness and ease only when taste won't be compromised. (If you do find yourself temporarily out of a fresh herb, use only about a third as much of the dried as you would of the fresh.)

There's no substitute, however, for freshly ground black pepper; keep a pepper mill handy. As freshly grated nutmeg can add a real flavor boost to many dishes, we try to keep a little nutmeg and a fine grater in the pantry as well.

Lately, we've taken to concocting some of our own spice mixtures, which allows for a wonderful degree of creative control over seasoning. Try making your own Fines Herbes (page 21) and Curry Powder (page 22).

HERB VINEGAR: See page 23.

JALAPEÑO PEPPERS: As we were writing this book, chopped jalapeño peppers in the jar appeared on the scene in our local produce aisle alongside the chopped gar-lic. Needless to say, this saves a tremendous amount of seeding, deveining, and chop-ping time (all of it spent attempting to avoid rubbing your eyes).

The precut variety of pepper precludes the need to stock up on fresh peppers, which invariably dry out before you use them up. The product we've purchased utilizes red jalapeño peppers, which provide a more colorful touch than the green peppers that are typically stocked whole.

JUICE: Freshly squeezed lemon and lime juice really do make a difference, and require virtually no extra effort beyond remembering to keep a supply on hand. If you substitute commercial orange juice for freshly squeezed, use a variety that is not made from concentrate.

When tomato juice is called for, choose a low-sodium variety.

MILK: We call for skim milk, buttermilk, and evaporated skim milk in our recipes. Buttermilk, contrary to the popular misconception, is made from skim milk and contains no butter. Compare nutrition labels for evaporated skim milks, which can vary in fat content even between different products from the same manufacturer.

PASTA: See page 16.

POLENTA: See page 18.

POTATOES: In some recipes, we use precut refrigerated or frozen potatoes to save time and effort. Read package labels carefully to ensure that what you are buying simply consists of precut potatoes (as opposed to products formed from mashed potatoes), to which only a little ascorbic acid has been added to prevent discoloration— and not a type made with oil, added flavorings, or an array of preservatives.

POULTRY: We use lean cuts of turkey and chicken, which are quite low in fat when properly trimmed, in many of our recipes. Keep a few simple guidelines in mind when shopping.

— When ground poultry is called for, avoid preground meat, which can contain a considerable amount of fat. Our recipes include directions for doing your own grinding in the food processor. Alternatively, you can select a lean cut and have your butcher trim and grind the meat.

— Turkey breast tenderloin, the leanest part of the breast trimmed of skin and fat, is readily available prepackaged.

- When buying smoked turkey, look for packages marked "smoked turkey breast," which contain intact turkey breast and not a pressed turkey product; be sure to remove the skin if it has not already been removed.
- Selecting among the varieties of smoked turkey sausage to find the ones lowest in fat requires reading product labels. Of the many smoked sausage products marked "low fat" or "reduced fat," only a few are made exclusively of turkey with no pork or other fatty additives. Compare fat counts and choose the lowest.
- When shopping for sliced turkey, choose a high-quality variety from lean turkey breast, prepackaged or freshly sliced at the deli counter.
- Buy skinless, boneless chicken breasts, trimmed of all visible fat, preferably from the butcher. (You need only look closely at some of the prepackaged commercial brands laden with gobs of fat to know what we mean.) A little chicken goes a long way in our recipes; it's worth the splurge to buy Amish or other free-range products.

RICE: Several brands of long-grain white rice are well within our guidelines for fat content if cooked without butter; we include directions for cooking the rice in individual recipes. (And, although it may raise an eyebrow or two regarding the relative fat content, we admit to hoarding containers of cooked rice from the occasional Chinese takeout dinner in our freezer to have on hand when we're absolutely slammed for time and want to pare down meal preparation even further.)

In recipes that call for Italian arborio rice, know that you can substitute other Spanish, Italian, or Japanese short-grain varieties. Do not, however, substitute long-grain rice. This is especially important in preparing any baked rice dish, as the volume of water called for has been calculated for short-grain rice.

ROASTED PEPPERS: For convenience, we use commercially prepared roasted peppers, found in the jar with the Italian goods in most markets. You can now buy both sweet roasted peppers and roasted jalapeño peppers; however the jalapeños are roasted whole, so they must be cored and seeded.

If you prefer, you can roast your own peppers, which can then be stored in the refrigerator for up to five days or frozen in heavy-duty plastic freezer bags for up to one month.

To roast peppers from scratch, preheat the broiler and line the rack with aluminum foil. Cut the peppers in half lengthwise, then core and seed them. Place them on the rack, cut side down, 2 to 3 inches from the heat source. Broil for about 5 minutes, until charred. Carefully transfer the peppers to an airtight plastic bag and let them cool for about 10 minutes, after which the skin should rub off easily.

SALT: We usually use coarse kosher salt in all but baking recipes. Readily available in most supermarkets, kosher salt has less sodium per measure than finer-grain table salt.

SEAFOOD: Seafood is a staple in our kitchen. It's low in fat, quick to prepare, flavorful, and perfectly suited to add just the needed panache to a quick and healthy entertaining menu.

— We prefer littleneck clams to larger varieties—they're sweeter, less likely to toughen when cooked, and make for a very abundant plate served up in the shell. Remember that clams are alive until cooked, necessitating a few extra precautionary steps. If you buy clams prepackaged in a plastic-wrapped Styrofoam container, punch a few holes in the plastic before putting it in the refrigerator to allow the clams to breathe. When ready to use, rinse the clams under cold running water, scrubbing the shells lightly if necessary to dislodge any residual sand and discarding clams that don't close when tapped, as well as any with broken shells. The clams should open naturally while cooking; toss any that don't.

— Our recipes are written for fresh mussels, not the frozen variety from New Zealand. For convenience, buy debearded mussels; they're usually packaged in mesh bags. Rinse them as you would clams, discarding those with broken shells, any that don't close under cold running water, and any that don't open while cooking.

— We usually choose bay scallops over the larger sea scallops when they

are available. Be aware that there is a certain gamble involved. Sea scallops are consistently good. Bay scallops vary in quality, but can't be equalled when they're in their prime. If substituting an equal weight of sea scallops for bay scallops, cut the scallops in quarters before cooking.

— We use cooked and shelled shrimp in most of our recipes to eliminate cooking, as well as peeling and deveining, at mealtime. Buy cooked shrimp at the market or cook them in quantity in advance, following the directions on page 15 for preparing Shrimp Stock, and freeze them for future use. Raw shrimp can also be purchased peeled and deveined in many markets.

— Use readily available cleaned squid rings, fresh or frozen, for convenience. Almost all squid sold in the United States arrives frozen from Asia or the Mediterranean. The only difference between the prepackaged rings in the seafood freezer case and those sold at the fish counter is that you won't need to defrost the latter. There should be no discernible odor as the squid thaws.

— We use extremely low-fat Pacific cod liberally. Avoid Atlantic cod, which is much higher in fat.

— We also make use of tilapia, a relative newcomer that's farm-raised. Tilapia is mild tasting, extremely low in fat, and virtually boneless when filleted.

SUN-DRIED TOMATOES: Sun-dried tomatoes can be purchased prepared (red or yellow tomatoes halved, red tomatoes chopped) or dried at home.

To dry your own tomatoes, preheat the oven to 170 degrees. Cut Italian plum tomatoes in half lengthwise and place them on a cookie sheet, cut side up. Bake for at least 6 hours (the time needed can vary quite a bit), until the tomatoes are dry, deep reddish brown in color, and still somewhat elastic. Do not allow them to blacken or become brittle. Let them cool completely and store in airtight containers.

TOMATOES: Although we use fresh tomatoes when time allows, many of our recipes call for canned tomatoes for convenience. (Canned tomatoes are actually preferable to hothouse tomatoes, since they are allowed to ripen longer on the vine; furthermore, they have been peeled.) We make full use of the burgeoning array of preseasoned diced tomatoes, which are not only easy to use but also save cooking time that would otherwise be needed for the flavors to meld.

Our favorite new discovery is Pomi brand strained tomatoes in a box, imported from Italy, which are nothing but pure strained tomatoes with no additives. They're particularly useful in the preparation of quick soups.

TORTILLAS: The fat content of tortillas varies widely; compare nutrition labels. Traditionally, only certain brands of yellow corn tortillas could be used in fat-free cooking. However, we've recently found white corn tortillas, as well as flour tortillas (stocked in refrigerator cases, usually in the dairy section) that are low enough in fat.

VEAL: We occasionally use small amounts of veal in our fat-free recipes. Buy veal scaloppine, which is a piece of meat from the leanest cut that's been pounded thin. If you want a bit of a splurge, know that veal can be substituted for chicken breast in many recipes, adding about a tenth of a gram of fat for every ounce used.

VEGETABLES: We use frozen rather than fresh in the case of vegetables that otherwise would require lengthy prepping, such as corn or peas, lengthy precooking, such as artichokes or squash, or that are highly seasonal, such as okra.

Remove the vegetables from the freezer and allow them to thaw before you begin meal preparation only when so instructed in the individual recipe. In many cases, recipes are written specifically so that vegetables added while still frozen will cook just long enough to retain the crunch of fresh vegetables.

For the Carrot Soufflé (page 174), we use another of our favorite new discoveries, frozen organic baby food. Don't be put off by the nomenclature; this is nothing more than pure carrots cooked in water and pureed, cutting preparation time down to minutes.

VEGETABLE STOCK: See page 14.

WHIPPED TOPPING: See page 24.

Equipment

FOOD PROCESSOR: It's hard to cook these days without a food processor, which pares many meal preparation chores to a fraction of the time that would otherwise be required. In some cases, a blender can be substituted, especially when working with a somewhat liquid mixture and when a very smooth consistency is desired.

GRATIN DISHES: You can readily substitute a nonstick 9-inch round cake pan for the more esoteric gratin dish; use a pan that's attractive enough to go from the oven to the dinner table.

MICROWAVE: In our pursuit of fast fat-free meals, we often rely on a microwave oven to precook the ingredients partially. In a few cases, we offer alternatives that fit readily into recipe preparation, such as boiling in water that has already been heated for a subsequent step in the recipe.

PRESSURE COOKER: We've recently rediscovered the pressure cooker, which can cut down considerably on the time involved in preparing long-cooking stews, beans, and stocks. The new lines of pressure cookers are particularly suited to quick preparation of fat-free meals, since they don't require the addition of oil or other superfluous fats.

SKILLETS: Use nonstick skillets that preclude the use of oil, preferably heavy-bottomed ones that will heat evenly and not warp over high heat. Choose pans with oven-safe handles that can go from cooktop to oven. We're particularly fond of skillets (and saucepans) with glass lids that allow you to monitor cooking without removing the covers.

WOKS: We use a nonstick wok because no oil need be added. Choose the appropriate wok for your cooktop; they now come flat-bottomed for electric cooktops as well as round-bottomed for gas ranges. Always preheat the wok before stir-frying so that the food will seal, remain crisp, and cook quickly; when beads of water dropped into the hot wok sizzle, it's ready. If you don't have a wok, use your largest nonstick skillet.

Chicken Stock

4 pounds chicken bones, with a few
    scraps of meat left on

3 carrots, trimmed and cut into chunks
    (unpeeled)

2 parsnips, trimmed and quartered
    lengthwise (unpeeled)

1 large yellow onion, cut into 1-inch
    chunks

5 stalks celery, trimmed and quartered

15 sprigs fresh flat-leaf parsley, ends
    trimmed

Water to cover above ingredients by 2
    inches (about 20 cups)

12 whole black peppercorns

Put the chicken bones, vegetables, and parsley in a large stockpot. Cover with water. Bring to a rapid boil over high heat, then skim the foamy residue off the top. Reduce the heat to low and simmer, uncovered, for about 4 hours, until the bones begin to disintegrate. Periodically skim the residue off the top.

Remove the pot from the heat. Discard all solid ingredients from the stock and strain the liquid into a large bowl. Add the peppercorns. Refrigerate, uncovered, for at least 2 to 3 hours. If refrigerating overnight, cover after 2 to 3 hours.

When you take the stock out of the refrigerator, use a large spoon to lift off as much as possible of the layer of fat that has settled on top. Using a dinner knife, scrape along the top of the stock to catch any additional small pieces of fat. Put the stock in a large pot and cook it over medium heat for 2 to 3 minutes, until it has turned from a gelatinous state back into liquid. Pour the liquefied stock through a strainer lined with a double layer of cheesecloth (to strain sediment) into a clean bowl.

YIELD = 6 TO 8 CUPS

Once the fat has been skimmed, good old-fashioned chicken stock is a fat-free cook's best friend! We recommend making your own stock in order to best control taste and fat content. It will keep for up to 3 days in the refrigerator and can be frozen in handy 2-cup portions in heavy-duty plastic freezer bags to have on hand for quick meal preparation.

By using a pressure cooker, you can cut down the cooking time to a little over 1 hour and eliminate the need to skim while cooking. To make this volume of stock, use at least an 8-quart capacity cooker, filled no more than two thirds full, and follow the manufacturer's directions.

If you use commercial chicken stock rather than making your own, refrigerate, skim, and strain it according to the directions below before proceeding to use the stock in a recipe.

Vegetable Stock

Flavorful homemade vegetable stock is always preferable to canned. When you have a bit of extra time, make a batch for future use. It will keep for up to 3 days in the refrigerator and can be frozen in 1 or 2-cup portions in heavy-duty plastic freezer bags. You can speed up cooking time to about 45 minutes by using a pressure cooker; see directions in the recipe for Chicken Stock on page 13.

When choosing commercial stock, compare nutrition labels, as some brands include ingredients that add fat to the stock.

1 large yellow onion, coarsely chopped

2 medium leeks, trimmed, rinsed, and sliced

2 tomatoes (or 6 plum tomatoes), coarsely chopped

4 carrots, peeled and coarsely chopped

4 cloves garlic, peeled

3 stalks celery, trimmed and sliced

10 sprigs fresh flat-leaf parsley, ends trimmed

6 whole black peppercorns

4 bay leaves

16 cups water

Combine all the ingredients in a large stockpot. Bring to a boil over medium-high heat. Reduce the heat to low and simmer gently, uncovered, for 2 hours.

Strain into a large bowl, pressing down on the vegetables to extract as much liquid as possible.

YIELD = 6 TO 8 CUPS

Shrimp Stock

2 pounds shrimp, in the shell   8 cups water

Peel and devein the shrimp, reserving the shells.

Bring the water to a boil in a large pot over high heat. Add the shrimp and the reserved shells to the pot. Reduce the heat to medium, cover, and cook for about 5 minutes, until both the shrimp and the shells are bright pink. With a slotted spoon, transfer the shrimp to a bowl and remove and discard the shells.

In heavy-duty plastic freezer bags, freeze the stock in 1- or 2-cup quantities and the shrimp in 4- to 6-ounce quantities.

YIELD = ABOUT 6 CUPS STOCK AND
1¾ POUNDS COOKED SHRIMP

Shrimp stock adds a wonderful accent to seafood recipes requiring stock. You can't buy it commercially prepared, but it is much faster to cook from scratch than other stocks, and its byproduct is a ready supply of cooked shrimp to stash in the freezer for future meals—or for a party!

Pasta

In many recipes, we call for readily available yolkless noodles, since it is still something of a challenge to find commercial pasta as low in fat. (Much of the dried pasta sold in supermarkets, even though it contains no egg, still exceeds our fat parameters; and fresh pasta typically is made with egg yolk.) For most of our recipes, you can readily substitute this almost fat-free homemade pasta for commercially made noodles.

The dough can be made in advance and stored in heavy-duty freezer storage bags for up to 1 month, or refrigerated for 3 to 5 days.

2 cups all-purpose flour	¾ cup nonfat liquid egg substitute

Put the flour into the bowl of a food processor. Pulse while adding the egg substitute. This will produce a soft ball of dough.

Turn the dough out onto a floured board and knead it a few times to form a glossy and elastic ball. Enclose it in plastic wrap and set it aside for 30 minutes.

Flour the rollers of a pasta machine. Cut the dough in quarters, flour all over, and flatten. Put the first piece through the largest opening on the pasta machine 3 times, folding the dough in half after each time through. Then put it through each successively smaller opening, until it has gone through the smallest. Repeat this process for the remaining 3 pieces of dough.

Put each of the thin sheets of dough through the wide cutters on the pasta machine. Hang and dry the strands of pasta for about 10 minutes. For homemade noodles, cut each strand into 2½- to 3-inch lengths and lay flat to dry on baking sheets that have been lined with clean, dry towels.

YIELD = 1 POUND

Gnocchi

1 pound Yukon Gold potatoes (about 3 potatoes)

5 cups cold water

1 large egg white

¾ cup all-purpose flour

Combine the potatoes and water in a medium saucepan over medium heat. Cook uncovered for 30 minutes. Drain, and remove the potato skins while still hot by rubbing with a clean dish towel. In a bowl, rice the peeled potatoes and allow them to cool for 2 to 3 minutes. Add the egg white and flour and mix with lightly floured hands, just until a cohesive soft dough is formed.

Break off small sections of dough and roll them out into 1-inch-thick ropes. Cut the ropes on the diagonal into ½-inch dumplings. Make a shallow incision in the middle of each with a sharp pointed knife.

Cook the gnocchi according to individual recipe directions.

YIELD = ABOUT 1 POUND

Anyone who can't yet find handy vacuum-packed gnocchi in their market can whip up a batch from scratch in less than an hour. The gnocchi will keep for about 3 days in the refrigerator. To freeze for up to 1 month, toss the dumplings in 1 tablespoon potato flour and seal them in heavy-duty freezer storage bags.

Polenta

This tasty Italian cornmeal makes a wonderful bed for stews, and can be served by itself as a first course as well. We're lucky enough to have ready-made polenta stocked by our local supermarket, but polenta is also quite easy to make at home. Removed from the loaf pan and wrapped in plastic wrap, the polenta will keep for up to 1 week in the refrigerator.

To serve, cut the loaf into 1/2-inch-thick slices and broil it for about 2 minutes per side, until lightly browned. (You can also brown the polenta on a nonstick stovetop grill.)

1⅓ cups skim milk

¼ cup buttermilk

½ teaspoon sugar

⅛ teaspoon salt

½ cup yellow cornmeal

½ tablespoon snipped fresh chives (optional)

2 cloves garlic, peeled (optional)

Vegetable oil cooking spray

In a small saucepan, combine the skim milk, buttermilk, sugar, and salt and cook over medium heat. Slowly whisk in the cornmeal. Reduce the heat to low and cook for about 5 minutes, stirring constantly, until the mixture is thick and smooth and comes away easily from the sides of the pan. Whisk in the chives or press in the garlic, if desired. Transfer to a 5¾-inch mini-loaf pan that has been sprayed lightly with vegetable oil cooking spray. Cover and refrigerate for 1 hour.

Prepare the polenta according to individual recipe directions.

YIELD = ABOUT 12 OUNCES

French Bread

¼ cup lukewarm water (105 to 115 degrees on an instant-read thermometer)

½ teaspoon sugar

1 packet quick-rise yeast

3 cups bread flour

½ teaspoon salt

¾ cup plus 2 tablespoons skim milk, at room temperature

½ teaspoon cornmeal, for dusting

1 large egg white, mixed with 1 tablespoon water

5 ice cubes

Put the water and sugar into a small bowl. Sprinkle the yeast on top and set aside for a few minutes, until the mixture is bubbly.

Combine the bread flour and salt in the bowl of a food processor and process for 1 minute. Scrape in the yeast mixture. Turn the machine back on and drizzle the skim milk through the feed tube until a dough ball forms, then process for 45 seconds to 1 minute more.

Put the ball in a bowl, cover with a moist towel, and place it in a warm (around 80 degrees) spot for about 1½ hours, until the dough has doubled in size.

Punch the dough down, fold it in, and remove it to a work surface that has been dusted with flour. Flatten the dough, shape it into a rectangle, and roll it up into a 14-inch loaf.

Transfer the loaf to a nonstick cookie sheet that has been dusted with the cornmeal. Cover again with the moist towel and set aside for about 1 hour more, until the dough no longer springs back to the touch.

Preheat the oven to 425 degrees.

Paint the loaf with the egg wash and make 4 diagonal slashes into the top. Put 3 of the ice cubes directly onto the bottom of the oven and bake the bread for 5 minutes.

Add the remaining ice cubes and bake for about 25 minutes more, until the bread has browned and sounds hollow when tapped.

Cool on a wire rack.

YIELD = ONE 14-INCH LOAF

Although you now can find some commercial French breads that are relatively low in fat, we still prefer baking our own when time allows, and we usually keep a loaf or two in the freezer. Wrapped in aluminum foil and placed in a heavy-duty plastic freezer bag, this French Bread will keep for up to 2 months.

Buttermilk Biscuits

We use these versatile, flaky biscuits in desserts and to accompany any of our soups served by themselves at lunchtime. They're also great to keep on hand for making a quick appetizer or snack. If you can't find the Armenian flatbread we use for various of our wraps in your market, spread the filling on these biscuits to make little sandwiches instead.

2½ cups all-purpose flour

1 tablespoon baking powder

1 teaspoon baking soda

¼ teaspoon salt

3 tablespoons nonfat cream cheese

2 tablespoons nonfat sour cream

1 cup buttermilk

Vegetable oil cooking spray

2 tablespoons skim milk

Preheat the oven to 400 degrees.

In a large mixing bowl, stir together the flour, baking powder, baking soda, and salt. Using a pastry blender or 2 dinner knives, cut in the cream cheese and sour cream. Stir in the buttermilk.

With lightly floured hands, gather the dough into a ball, knead in the crumbs, and transfer it to a floured surface. Roll it out to a thickness of ½ inch. With a glass or a cookie cutter, cut out eight 2½-inch circles.

Spray a nonstick baking sheet once lightly with the vegetable oil spray and spread the oil over the surface. Put the circles on the sheet and brush them with the skim milk. Bake for about 12 minutes, until lightly browned. Remove the biscuits from the oven and let them cool.

YIELD = 8 BISCUITS

Fines Herbes

2 tablespoons dried thyme

2 tablespoons dried winter savory

2 tablespoons dried oregano

1 tablespoon dried rosemary

1 teaspoon dried marjoram

1 teaspoon rubbed sage

1 teaspoon dried basil

YIELD = ½ CUP

We use this classic seasoning blend constantly. It's great on poultry, seafood, or salads. Remember to store seasonings in opaque containers, in which they will remain fresh and flavorful from 6 months to 1 year.

Curry Powder

Pungent seasoning blends such as curry powder produce robust and aromatic fat-free dishes. There's no such thing as the definitive curry powder; a smidgen more or less of any of the basic spices that comprise the mix will change its character subtly. After much experimentation, this blend has become our favorite. Use it as a point of departure in your own fat-free kitchen.

1 tablespoon plus 1 teaspoon ground coriander

2 teaspoons ground cumin

2 teaspoons ground turmeric

2 teaspoons celery seed

1 teaspoon ground ginger

½ teaspoon freshly ground black pepper

YIELD = A SCANT ¼ CUP

Tarragon White Wine Vinegar

4 to 6 sprigs fresh tarragon   3 cups white wine vinegar

Rinse and dry the tarragon.

Place the herbs in a 750-ml. clamp jar or a clean wine bottle. Add the vinegar, leaving at least ¼ inch of air at the top. Seal and set aside in a cool, dark place to steep for about 2 weeks before using.

YIELD = 3 CUPS

This is our favorite herb vinegar, and there's always a bottle close by in our kitchen. We use it in salads and soups and to add flavor without fat to an endless array of dishes. The vinegar has a shelf life of at least 1 year; store it out of direct sunlight.

Creamy Whipped Topping

We love this simple, fat-free
alternative to whipped cream.
You can vary the liqueur used
to suit just about any dessert.
The topping is best used
within an hour of preparation.

1 cup evaporated skim milk, well chilled   1 tablespoon liqueur

Place a metal mixing bowl and the beaters from an electric mixer into the freezer to chill.

Pour the evaporated milk into the chilled bowl. Beat with the chilled beaters at high speed until frothy. Drizzle in the liqueur and continue to beat to soft peaks.

YIELD = ABOUT 1 CUP

Menus

for

Entertaining

Cod with Tomato-Basil Salsa
Roasted Garlic Potatoes
Wilted Zucchini

〜

*C*lassic flavor combinations colorfully presented, these recipes comprise a restaurant-quality meal that can be prepared at home easily. The presentation is stunning—a centerpiece of white fish, drizzled with a basil and tomato salsa and served alongside pale green zucchini and potatoes dotted with dark reddish-brown roasted garlic.

99% FAT-FREE FAST STRATEGY:
1. Preheat the oven. Meanwhile, prep and salt the zucchini; set aside.
2. Prep the potatoes and put them in the oven to bake.
3. When the potatoes are almost halfway done, season and bake the cod fillets; meanwhile, make the salsa and preheat a skillet.
4. Cook the zucchini in the hot skillet.

Wilted Zucchini

12 ounces zucchini (about 2 zucchini)
2 teaspoons coarse kosher salt

Vegetable oil cooking spray
Freshly ground black pepper to taste

Trim and cut the zucchini into thin rounds. Transfer to a colander, salt, and let sit for at least 15 minutes.

Preheat a medium nonstick skillet over high heat. Pat the zucchini rounds dry with paper toweling and spray twice lightly with cooking spray. Cook in the hot skillet, stirring frequently, for about 2 minutes, until the zucchini begins to brown. Season to taste with black pepper.

YIELD = 4 SERVINGS

Fat per serving = 0.30 g.

Calories per serving = 2.0

If you should be interrupted mid–menu, don't worry; the longer the zucchini sits in the salt, the better. For a colorful twist, substitute a medley of green, red, and white peppercorns for the black pepper.

Roasted Garlic Potatoes

We've long used the prechopped garlic sold in jars in supermarkets to save precious minutes in preparing meals, and were delighted recently to discover that you can now buy prechopped roasted garlic as well.

12 ounces small red potatoes (about 4 potatoes)

1 tablespoon minced roasted garlic (precut)

¼ cup water

Preheat the oven to 450 degrees. Line a 9-inch pie pan with aluminum foil.

Quarter each potato.

Place the potatoes into the pan, skin side down, and sprinkle with the garlic. Pour the water into the bottom of the pan, around the potatoes. Cover and bake in the center of the oven for about 20 minutes, until fork-tender.

YIELD = 4 SERVINGS

Fat per serving = 0.07 g.

Calories per serving = 56.4

Cod with Tomato-Basil Salsa

Four 6-ounce Pacific cod fillets

Salt and freshly ground black pepper to taste

1 clove garlic

8 ounces Italian plum tomatoes (about 2 tomatoes)

½ cup packed basil leaves

½ teaspoon coarse kosher salt

2 tablespoons freshly squeezed lime juice

Pinch of cayenne pepper

Preheat the oven to 450 degrees. Line a baking pan with aluminum foil.

Season the fillets all over with salt and black pepper. Place in the baking pan and bake for about 12 minutes, until cooked through.

Meanwhile, peel and smash the garlic and core and cut each tomato into 8 chunks. Combine the garlic, tomatoes, basil, kosher salt, lime juice, and cayenne in a food processor. Pulse to a chunky puree.

Serve ¼ cup salsa atop each fillet.

YIELD = 4 SERVINGS

Fat per serving = 0.93 g.

Calories per serving = 149.5

Buy Pacific cod, which has by far the lowest fat content of any variety on the market. For the salsa, use plum tomatoes, whose thin skins and paucity of seeds preclude the need to peel and seed.

Steamed Mahimahi in Tomato Syrup
Broiled Portobello Salad with Blue Cheese Dressing

⁓

*T*his is upscale dinner-party fare that almost no one can believe is virtually fat-free. The elegant tomato syrup atop the moist steamed mahimahi has a slightly sweet and sour accent, lent by the inclusion of rice wine vinegar and brown sugar. The creamy dressing on the portobello salad has a robust blue cheese flavor derived from the use of a surprisingly modest amount of cheese.

Accompanied by just a loaf of bread, the mahimahi makes a nice light lunch, while the salad can be served up with Onion Soup (page 61) for a substantial midday meal.

99% FAT-FREE FAST STRATEGY:

1. Preheat the broiler.
2. Make the tomato syrup. While it reduces, make the blue cheese dressing and prep and microwave the portobello mushrooms.
3. Put water up to boil for steaming. Meanwhile, prep the snow peas and shallot. Chop the vegetable topping for the salad in a food processor and heat in a microwave.
4. While the fish steams, arrange the portobello salad for broiling, preheat a skillet, and trim and rinse the chard.
5. Cook the chard in the hot skillet.
6. Broil the portobello salad.
7. Plate the fish atop the wilted chard and drizzle with the syrup.

Steamed Mahimahi in Tomato Syrup

¼ cup rice wine vinegar

2 tablespoons light brown sugar

¾ cup reduced-sodium tomato juice

2 pieces fresh ginger (each about the size
    of a quarter)

Four 4-ounce mahimahi fillets

12 ounces red chard (about 1 bunch)

In a small saucepan, combine the vinegar, brown sugar, tomato juice, and ginger. Bring to a boil over high heat and boil until the volume of the mixture is reduced to ½ cup, about 10 minutes. Remove and discard the ginger.

Position a wide, shallow steamer basket over rapidly boiling water. Place the fish fillets onto a plate in a single layer and set the plate into the steamer basket. Steam for about 8 minutes, until the fish is cooked through and no longer pink in the center.

Preheat a medium nonstick skillet over medium-high heat. Trim, break up (about 6 cups), and rinse the chard. Add the chard, while still damp, to the hot pan. Cook just long enough to wilt, 45 to 60 seconds.

Divide the chard among 4 dinner plates. Top each with a fish fillet and drizzle with about 2 tablespoons of the tomato syrup.

YIELD = 4 SERVINGS

Fat per serving = 0.85 g.

Calories per serving = 144.2

Blue Cheese Dressing

We use this simple, silky concoction to finish dumplings in our Gnocchi with Blue Cheese Dressing (page 162) and for our Couscous Salad (page 78). It works equally well with fruit salads.

¼ cup nonfat cottage cheese

½ tablespoon blue cheese

½ tablespoon skim milk

Combine all the ingredients in a food processor or blender and puree until the mixture is smooth and creamy, about 1 minute.

YIELD = ABOUT ¼ CUP

Fat per tablespoon = 0.60 g.

Calories per tablespoon = 14.4

Broiled Portobello Salad

6 ounces portobello mushrooms (about four 4-inch-diameter stemmed mushrooms)

1 ounce snow peas

1 shallot

2 baby-cut carrots

Salt and freshly ground black pepper to taste

¼ cup Blue Cheese Dressing (page 32)

In lieu of microwaving the mushrooms, you can steam them for 1 to 2 minutes before steaming the fish.

Preheat the broiler. Line a broiler tray with aluminum foil.

Trim and clean the mushrooms. Place in a single layer on a microwave-safe plate, cover loosely with plastic wrap, and microwave at full power until they're soft and just beginning to steam, about 1 minute. Place them stem side up on the prepared broiler tray.

Trim and halve the snow peas (about ¼ cup). Peel and halve the shallot. Combine the snow peas, shallot, and carrots in a food processor. Pulse about 15 times to finely chop. Transfer to a microwave-safe bowl, cover loosely with plastic wrap, and microwave at full power until steaming, about 1 minute.

Mound 1 tablespoon of the chopped vegetables in the center of each mushroom. Salt and pepper to taste. Pour 1 tablespoon of the blue cheese dressing over each.

Broil for about 1 minute, until bubbly and lightly browned.

YIELD = 4 SERVINGS

Fat per serving = 0.70 g. (including dressing)

Calories per serving = 27.9 (including dressing)

Gazpacho

Vegetable and Seafood Paella

Watercress and Carrot Salad

~

$\mathcal{A}$ great menu for entertaining, these recipes yield a meal that is as substantial as it is elegant. We've shortened preparation time for the paella considerably by partially cooking it on the stovetop before baking, as well as by using stock that has first been brought to a boil. Similarly, we start with cooked, shelled shrimp to save shelling and deveining time. Don't be deterred by the somewhat lengthy ingredient list; it actually entails very little in the way of hands-on preparation.

If you want to serve the gazpacho first, remove the paella from the oven and cover it to keep warm. The gazpacho can also serve as the main component of a satisfying lunch for four.

99% FAT-FREE FAST STRATEGY:

1. Preheat the oven. Meanwhile, prep the paella ingredients and bring the stock to a boil.
2. Start the paella. While it finishes cooking on the stovetop, prep the vegetables for the gazpacho.
3. Transfer the paella to the oven to bake.
4. Make and chill the gazpacho. Chill the salad plates.
5. While the paella bakes and the gazpacho chills, make the salad.
6. Garnish the paella and gazpacho.

Vegetable and Seafood Paella

3¹/₂ cups shrimp, chicken, or vegetable
    stock (see Pantry)

3 ounces sweet roasted peppers (preroasted)

One 14-ounce can diced tomatoes

1 pound Pacific cod fillets

4 ounces cooked, peeled medium shrimp

1 cup chopped white onion (precut)

2 teaspoons chopped garlic (precut)

1 tablespoon water

2 cups arborio rice

¹/₂ cup dry white wine

¹/₄ teaspoon dried thyme

¹/₄ teaspoon saffron threads

¹/₈ teaspoon cayenne pepper

One 9-ounce package frozen artichoke
    hearts, thawed

1 cup frozen butter beans

¹/₂ cup frozen baby peas

1 lemon, cut in wedges

1 tablespoon minced fresh flat-leaf parsley

Preheat the oven to 325 degrees. In a medium saucepan, bring the stock to a boil over medium heat. Rinse and drain the roasted peppers and drain the tomatoes. Chop the peppers (about ¹/₃ cup). Chunk the cod and cut the shrimp in half crosswise.

In a nonstick paella pan, a 12-inch nonstick skillet with an ovenproof handle, or a well-seasoned 12-inch cast-iron skillet, combine the onion, garlic, and water. Sauté over medium-high heat for 1 to 2 minutes, until the water has completely evaporated. Add the roasted peppers and tomatoes and stir for about 30 seconds, until blended. Stir in the rice. Add the boiling stock, the wine, and the herbs and spices; stir to mix. Bring back to a boil, reduce the heat to medium, and cook for 5 minutes.

Stir in the artichokes, butter beans, peas, cod, and shrimp. Transfer the pan to the oven and bake for 15 minutes. Garnish with a circle of lemon wedges and sprinkle with the parsley.

Serve about 2 cups per person.

YIELD = 6 SERVINGS

Fat per serving = 0.80 g.

Calories per serving = 332.7

For this paella—a dish named after the large, shallow pan in which it traditionally is cooked—we prefer the flavor lent by shrimp stock, but chicken or vegetable stock can be substituted if you don't have any shrimp stock on hand. We call for arborio rice, but you can substitute any other Italian, Spanish or Japanese short-grain white rice.

Gazpacho

Instead of thickening our gazpacho with oil and bread, as is typical, we use extra veggies—including the wonderful boxed variety of pure strained tomatoes with no additives, imported from Italy.

3 ounces yellow onion (about 1 small onion)

1¼ pounds hothouse cucumber (about 1 cucumber)

6 ounces green bell pepper (about 1 small pepper)

2½ cups boxed strained tomatoes (such as Pomi brand)

⅓ cup red wine vinegar

¼ teaspoon hot sauce

½ teaspoon salt

⅛ teaspoon cayenne pepper (optional)

Snipped fresh chives for garnish

Peel and cut the onion into 8 chunks and the cucumber into 16 chunks. Trim and cut the bell pepper into 8 chunks.

Combine the onion, cucumber, bell pepper, and tomatoes in a food processor and process to very small pieces. (Do not puree.)

Transfer to a mixing bowl. Stir in the vinegar, hot sauce, salt, and, if desired, cayenne. Cover and chill for at least 10 minutes.

Serve 1 cup in each of 6 soup bowls and garnish with the chives.

YIELD = 6 SERVINGS

Fat per serving = 0.21 g.

Calories per serving = 55.7

Watercress and Carrot Salad

1 teaspoon anchovy paste

½ teaspoon Dijon mustard

3 tablespoons white balsamic vinegar

3 tablespoons light corn syrup

6 ounces watercress (about 1 small bunch)

1½ cups shredded carrots (precut)

Chill 6 salad plates.

In a small bowl, whisk the anchovy paste and mustard. Add the vinegar and corn syrup and whisk until the mixture is thick and smooth.

Cut the thick stems from the watercress and roughly chop the leaves (about 1½ cups). Divide the watercress among the chilled salad plates. Mound ¼ cup of the carrots in the center of each, and drizzle about 1 tablespoon of dressing over each salad.

YIELD = 6 SERVINGS

Fat per serving = 0.24 g.

Calories per serving = 48.0

We developed this fat-free twist on a traditional Spanish carrot and anchovy salad to complement the flavor of the paella.

Garlic Shiitake Soup

Turkey Fricassee with Broiled Polenta Cakes

⁓

$\mathcal{A}$ fricassee, like a cacciatore, is usually a long-cooking stew. By slicing the meat into thin strips and using preseasoned canned tomatoes, we cut down the cooking time for this recipe significantly. It's served over polenta cakes, which provide a nice contrast in texture and become even more flavorful as they absorb the sauce.

We usually serve the soup after prepping all menu ingredients, but before starting hands-on cooking of the fricassee. Its pungent garlic and mushroom flavor complements the fricassee well, but the soup can also be paired easily with other entrées. Try it with our Grilled Vegetable Hoagie with Garlic Spread (page 149).

99% FAT-FREE FAST STRATEGY:

1. Prep the shiitake mushrooms.
2. Start the soup. While it simmers, prep the turkey, onion, and celery for the fricassee.
3. Transfer the contents of the soup pan to a blender and puree with additional stock. Return to the pan and finish cooking, mixing in the mushrooms and other additional ingredients. Meanwhile, preheat the broiler.
4. Preheat a skillet.
5. Start the fricassee in the hot skillet, adding ingredients as it cooks. Remove from the heat and cover to keep warm.
6. Broil the polenta.
7. Place two slices of polenta on each of four plates and top each with about 1/4 cups of turkey fricassee.

Garlic Shiitake Soup

4 ounces fresh shiitake mushrooms (about 8 mushrooms)

1 tablespoon plus 1 teaspoon minced roasted garlic (precut)

½ cup chopped white onion (precut)

One 8-ounce package sliced white button mushrooms

1½ cups chicken stock (see Pantry)

½ teaspoon chopped fresh thyme

2 tablespoons brandy

1½ cups evaporated skim milk

½ teaspoon salt

Freshly ground black pepper to taste

Trim, clean, and slice the shiitake mushrooms (about 1 packed cup); set aside.

In a large saucepan, combine the garlic, onion, white button mushrooms, and ½ cup of the chicken stock. Bring to a boil over high heat. Reduce the heat to medium, cover, and simmer for about 5 minutes, until the mushrooms can be mashed easily.

Transfer the contents of the pan to a blender. Add the remaining cup of chicken stock, and puree for 10 seconds. Scrape down the sides of the blender with a rubber spatula and puree for 20 seconds more.

Return the puree to the saucepan and add the shiitakes, thyme, and brandy. Cook over medium heat until the mixture starts to bubble. Add the evaporated milk and cook for about 2 minutes, just until steaming, taking care not to allow the soup to boil. Add the salt and pepper. Ladle 1 cup into each of 4 soup bowls.

YIELD = 4 SERVINGS

Fat per serving = 0.53 g.

Calories per serving = 136.5

We puree convenient and fast-cooking presliced white button mushrooms to thicken the soup, adding the considerably more costly shiitakes intact. Heat only until steaming after adding the evaporated skim milk, otherwise the soup will separate and curdle.

Premade polenta is beginning to turn up on supermarket shelves all over the country, in plain as well as seasoned form. You can also make your own from scratch (see Pantry) if you're so inclined, or if it is not yet available in your market.

Turkey Fricassee with Broiled Polenta Cakes

10 ounces turkey breast tenderloin

4 ounces yellow onion (about 1 small onion)

2 ounces celery (about 2 small stalks)

One 14½-ounce can diced tomatoes with garlic, basil, and oregano

1 cup shredded carrot (precut)

2 tablespoons water

1 teaspoon paprika

½ teaspoon salt

⅛ teaspoon ground black pepper

¾ cup dry white wine

12 ounces polenta (see sidebar)

Thinly slice the turkey (about 1 cup plus 2 tablespoons). Trim and thinly slice the onion (about ¾ cup) and the celery (about ½ cup). Drain the tomatoes.

Preheat the broiler and line a broiler tray with aluminum foil.

Preheat a medium nonstick skillet over medium-high heat. Combine the onion, celery, carrot, and water in the hot skillet and stir. Cover and cook for about 2 minutes, until the vegetables have begun to soften. Add the turkey and paprika and cook for 1 to 2 minutes, stirring constantly, until the meat is no longer pink. Stir in the tomatoes, salt, black pepper, and wine. Continue to cook for about 1 minute more, stirring constantly, until bubbly. Cover and remove from the heat.

Cut the polenta into eight ½-inch-thick slices and place on the prepared broiler tray. Broil for about 2 minutes per side, until lightly browned.

For each serving, top 2 slices of polenta with 1¼ cups of fricassee.

YIELD = 4 SERVINGS

Fat per serving = 1.00 g.

Calories per serving = 222.9

Shrimp, Leek, and Asparagus Risotto
Squid Salad

~

We received so many compliments on the risottos in our first *99% Fat-Free Cookbook*, especially the curried lobster recipe, that we just had to include a risotto in this edition. A bit of tinkering here and there has produced the even creamier curried risotto featured in this menu, which we pair with a crisp and cool squid salad. Compose the salad first and let it chill while you make the risotto.

The flavor of the risotto will vary greatly with the use of different curry powders. We like the aromatic and zesty version we make ourselves (see Pantry). Commercial curry powders can range from relatively mild supermarket varieties (for which you might want to boost the quantity to 1/4 teaspoons) to spicy Madras curries found in Indian groceries and spice shops.

99% FAT-FREE FAST STRATEGY:
1. Make the salad and refrigerate to chill.
2. Prep the leek, asparagus, and shrimp for the risotto.
3. While bringing the stock mixture to a boil, microwave the asparagus and preheat a saucepan.
4. Sauté the leek in the hot saucepan, then the rice.
5. Incrementally stir stock into the rice, add the remaining ingredients, and finish cooking the risotto.
6. Plate the salad atop the lettuce mixture.

Squid Salad

Just a couple of years ago, it was usually necessary to buy whole squid. Today, thankfully, cleaned squid rings are readily available in supermarkets, fresh or frozen. Take care not to overcook the squid, which is done in less than a minute.

3 ounces celery (about 2 stalks)

1 tablespoon drained capers

2 tablespoons drained sliced pimiento

½ teaspoon minced garlic (precut)

1 teaspoon salt

6 ounces cleaned squid rings (about ¾ cup)

12 drops hot sauce

¼ cup freshly squeezed lemon juice

4 cups romaine lettuce and radicchio salad mix

Trim and chop the celery (about ½ cup). Combine in a bowl with the capers, pimiento, and garlic.

Bring a medium saucepan half filled with water to a boil over high heat. Add the salt and the squid. Cook for about 30 seconds, until the squid turns opaque and begins to firm. Transfer the squid to the bowl. Add the hot sauce to the lemon juice, and add the combination to the bowl. Stir to mix. Cover and refrigerate until ready to serve.

Serve a generous ⅓ cup of the chilled salad on each of 4 plates, atop 1 cup of the romaine and radicchio mix.

YIELD = 4 SERVINGS

Fat per serving = 0.87 g.

Calories per serving = 56.8

Shrimp, Leek, and Asparagus Risotto

4 ounces leek (about 1 thin leek)

4 ounces asparagus (5 to 7 spears)

12 ounces cooked, shelled medium shrimp

3½ cups chicken stock (see Pantry)

1 cup clam juice or shrimp stock (see Pantry)

1⅓ cups arborio rice

1 teaspoon curry powder (see Pantry)

Trim the leek to light green and white parts only. Cut in half lengthwise, clean, and slice thin (about ⅔ cup). Trim and cut the asparagus into 1-inch pieces (about 1 cup). Cut each shrimp crosswise into thirds.

In a medium saucepan, combine the chicken stock and the clam juice or shrimp stock. Bring to a boil over high heat. (Lower the heat to medium once you begin to add the liquid to the risotto.) Meanwhile, place the asparagus in a microwave-safe container, cover loosely with plastic wrap, and microwave at full power for about 1 minute, until the asparagus are bright green. Remove and set aside.

Preheat a large, heavy-bottomed saucepan over medium heat. Put the leek in the hot pan and sauté dry for 2½ to 3 minutes, until soft. Add the rice and cook for about 1 minute more, stirring constantly, until lightly browned. Add 1 cup of the hot stock mixture, raise the heat to medium-high, and cook, stirring constantly, until the stock has been absorbed. Continue to add hot stock, ½ cup at a time, cooking and stirring until it has been absorbed between additions. When you have added 4 cups, stir the asparagus, shrimp, and curry powder into the risotto. Add the last ½ cup of stock and cook, stirring, until absorbed. This risotto should take 15 to 20 minutes to prepare.

Serve about 1½ cups per person.

YIELD = 4 SERVINGS

Fat per serving = 0.92 g.

Calories per serving = 191.5

Never make risotto in a nonstick pan; there's something about the coated surface that inhibits the stirring rhythm that's integral to preparation. In lieu of microwaving the asparagus, you can parboil it for 3 to 4 minutes in the water in which you have just cooked the squid rings; run under cold water and set aside until ready to use.

Michael Silverstein's Penne with Asparagus and Smoked Turkey

Navy Bean and Shrimp Salad

—

When we served penne with asparagus to our discerning dining companion Michael Silverstein, he said it was good, but would be better with the addition of a bit of smoked turkey—and he was right! For an indulgent finishing touch, garnish each bowl of penne with two anchovies (from which you have blotted excess oil), arranged as an **X**.

Since the refreshing navy bean and shrimp salad is prepared first and eaten at room temperature, it can be served alongside the penne or before you proceed with preparing the rest of the meal. You can also adapt the penne for a first course simply by cutting the recipe in half.

99% FAT-FREE FAST STRATEGY:
1. Make the salad.
2. Put a pot of water over high heat; while the water comes to a boil, prep the asparagus and turkey.
3. Cook the asparagus in the boiling water. Remove, rinse, and drain.
4. Cook the penne in the boiling water; meanwhile, sauté the garlic in a skillet, add the turkey and stock to the skillet, and cook.
5. Drain the penne and toss the asparagus and pasta with the turkey mixture.

Navy Bean and Shrimp Salad

One 15-ounce can navy beans

3 ounces sweet roasted peppers (preroasted)

8 ounces Italian plum tomatoes (about 2 tomatoes)

6 ounces arugula (about 1 bunch)

5 ounces cooked, peeled medium shrimp

1 cup sliced white button mushrooms (precut)

¾ teaspoon rubbed sage

½ teaspoon dried basil

¼ teaspoon ground black pepper

⅛ teaspoon salt

2 tablespoons freshly squeezed lemon juice

Rinse and drain the beans and roasted peppers. Core and chop the tomatoes (about 1 cup). Chop the peppers (about ⅓ cup) and arugula (about 3 cups). Cut the shrimp in half crosswise.

Combine all the ingredients in a large bowl and mix thoroughly. Serve a scant 1 cup on each of 6 salad plates.

YIELD = 6 SERVINGS

Fat per serving = 0.88 g.

Calories per serving = 109.8

Trim the asparagus on the diagonal to about the same length as the penne. The addition of the bright green spears not only provides an interesting visual contrast to the pale penne, but also allows for more abundant portions since the asparagus is much lower in fat than the pasta. Here we use chicken stock, rather than the usual olive oil or cream, to lend the asparagus a coat that glistens and the penne a silky gloss.

Michael Silverstein's Penne with Asparagus and Smoked Turkey

1 pound asparagus (20 to 28 spears)
4½ ounces skinless smoked turkey breast
8 ounces penne pasta
½ tablespoon chopped garlic (precut)

2 tablespoons water
½ cup chicken stock (see Pantry)
Salt and freshly ground black pepper to taste

Bring a large pot of water to a boil over high heat.

Meanwhile, trim the asparagus and cut them on the diagonal into 2-inch pieces (about 3 cups). Cut the turkey into julienne strips (about ¾ cup).

Add the asparagus spears to the boiling water, bring back to a boil, and cook for 3 to 4 minutes, until they're bright green and tender but still firm. Transfer the asparagus to a colander with a slotted spoon, run briefly under cold water, and set aside to drain.

Add the penne to the boiling water and cook to desired tenderness, about 10 minutes.

When the pasta has cooked halfway, combine the garlic and water in a large nonstick skillet over medium heat, stirring until the water has evaporated. Stir in the turkey breast and chicken stock. Cover, reduce the heat to medium-low, and cook for 3 minutes.

Drain the penne in the colander with the asparagus. Add the penne and asparagus to the turkey mixture and toss to mix, coat the pasta, and heat thoroughly. Season with salt and pepper.

Divide equally among 6 dinner plates.

YIELD = 6 SERVINGS

Fat per serving = 0.88 g.

Calories per serving = 173.1

Steamed Cod and Vegetable Salad
with Mushroom Dressing

This simple, elegant one-plate meal is a favorite of ours for last-minute entertaining. It's a dish we never tire of, sometimes substituting skate, red snapper, or halibut for the cod.

Paired with a loaf of crusty bread and a crisp, dry white wine, the salad makes a satisfying dinner (which we like to finish with Pear-Ginger Sorbet, page 184)—yet it's light enough to serve as luncheon or brunch fare. To serve as a first course, reduce the amount of fish to about 3 ounces per person, and omit the potatoes and green beans.

99% FAT-FREE FAST STRATEGY:

1. Start the mushroom dressing; while the mushrooms boil, prep the potatoes and green beans. Put water up to boil for steaming.
2. Strain the mushrooms and finish the dressing. Cover and set aside.
3. Steam the potatoes and green beans; prep the mushrooms and roasted peppers while the potatoes and green beans steam.
4. Steam the fish fillets; meanwhile, preheat a skillet, cook the mushrooms and roasted peppers in the hot skillet, and warm the dressing.
5. Compose and dress the salads.

Mushroom Dressing

1¼ cups water

1 ounce dried shiitake mushrooms (also
    called black Chinese mushrooms;
    about 6 large mushrooms)

1 shallot

¼ cup bourbon

¼ cup balsamic vinegar

In a small saucepan, combine the water and mushrooms. Bring to a boil over medium-high heat. Meanwhile, mince the shallot. Boil the mushrooms for about 8 minutes, until they have softened and the liquid has reduced.

Fit a sieve over a measuring cup and pour in the contents of the pan. (You should have about ½ cup mushroom stock; squeeze the mushrooms to release additional liquid if needed.) Reserve the mushrooms, rinse out the saucepan, and return the stock to the pan. Add the bourbon, shallot, and vinegar. Bring back to a boil over medium-high heat and boil for 1 minute. Remove the pan from the heat, cover, and set aside.

Warm just before serving.

YIELD = ABOUT 1 CUP

Fat per tablespoon = 0.02 g.

Calories per tablespoon = 24.2

In this unique dressing, the rich, smoky taste of bourbon, from which the alcohol has been burned off, blends wonderfully with the concentrated flavor of the reduced mushroom cooking liquid. We use it in our Chicken Scaloppine with Polenta (page 93) as well.

Steamed Cod and Vegetable Salad

1 pound new red potatoes (about 12 potatoes)

4 ounces green beans (about 24 beans)

One 12-ounce jar sweet roasted peppers

Four 5-ounce cod fillets

2 tablespoons balsamic vinegar

4 cups bitter greens salad mix

1 cup Mushroom Dressing (page 48)

Snipped fresh chives for garnish (optional)

Cut the potatoes in half and trim the green beans. Rinse and drain the roasted peppers.

Position a wide, shallow steamer basket over a pot of rapidly boiling water. Put the potatoes into the basket and steam for 5 minutes. Add the green beans and steam for about 5 minutes more, until the beans are bright green and the potatoes fork tender. While the vegetables are steaming, stem and slice the mushrooms reserved from preparing the dressing and cut the roasted peppers lengthwise into strips. Transfer the steamed potatoes and green beans to a sheet of aluminum foil and enclose to keep warm.

Place the fish fillets onto a plate in a single layer and set the plate into the steamer basket. Steam until the fish turns white and opaque, 3 to 4 minutes. Meanwhile, preheat a medium nonstick skillet over high heat. Add the mushrooms, roasted peppers, and vinegar. Cook for about 1 minute, until the liquid has been absorbed and the vegetables heated.

Divide the bitter greens among 4 dinner plates. Scatter about ⅓ cup of the mushroom and pepper mixture over the center of each, and top with a fish fillet. Arrange the potatoes and green beans around the fish. Drizzle about ¼ cup of the dressing over each plate and garnish, if desired, with chives.

YIELD = 4 SERVINGS

Fat per serving = 0.97 g. (including dressing)

Calories per serving = 306.8 (including dressing)

Spicy Squash Soup

Ann Bloomstrand's Baked Fish in Red Chard

*Y*our dinner guests will love the individual gratins of orange roughy, wrapped with delicate French green beans and carrots in colorful red chard. It's the invention of our buddy Ann Bloomstrand, our partner in many a culinary experiment. The recipe is a considerably quicker and easier alternative to steaming fish in parchment or puff pastry, to say nothing of the relative fat content.

The squash soup, which contains a complex, Southwestern–style medley of spices, provides an interesting contrast to the more mildly seasoned gratin. We usually serve the soup while the fish bakes.

99% FAT–FREE FAST STRATEGY:

1. Start the soup.
2. Mix additional ingredients into the soup, bring to a boil, and let simmer.
3. While the soup simmers, prep ingredients for the fish dish and microwave the haricots verts.
4. Assemble the gratins.
5. Bake the gratins.

Spicy Squash Soup

3 cups vegetable stock (see Pantry)

One 12-ounce package frozen cooked winter squash

¾ cup chopped white onion (precut)

¼ teaspoon chopped jalapeño pepper (precut)

1 teaspoon ground cumin

¾ teaspoon paprika

½ teaspoon ground coriander

½ tablespoon freshly squeezed lime juice

Salt and freshly ground black pepper to taste

2 tablespoons chopped fresh cilantro

In a large saucepan, combine 2½ cups of the vegetable stock and the squash over high heat.

Combine the remaining ½ cup of stock, the onion, and the jalapeño pepper in a blender and puree until smooth, about 5 seconds. Stir the mixture into the pan with the squash. Add the cumin, paprika, and coriander. Bring to a boil, then reduce the heat to medium and simmer for 7 minutes, until heated through and steaming.

Stir in the lime juice. Season with salt and pepper. Ladle 1 cup into each of 4 soup bowls and garnish each with ½ tablespoon cilantro.

YIELD = 4 SERVINGS

Fat per serving = 0.24 g.

Calories per serving = 59.4

By starting with frozen cooked squash, instead of peeling, cooking, and pureeing fresh squash, we save a minimum of 45 minutes. There is no need to thaw frozen ingredients used in soup making; they will thaw as the soup cooks. Use red jalapeño pepper, which lends a colorful accent to the soup, if possible.

Choose the prettiest leaves of chard you can find!

Ann Bloomstrand's Baked Fish in Red Chard

6 ounces red chard (about 4 large leaves)

9 ounces orange roughy fillets

4 ounces haricots verts (French green beans)

½ cup shredded carrots (precut)

¼ cup chopped white onion (precut)

2 tablespoons chopped fresh chervil

½ cup dry white wine

1 teaspoon minced roasted garlic (precut)

1 teaspoon Dijon mustard

Salt and freshly ground black pepper to taste

Preheat the oven to 400 degrees.

Trim the chard and line each of 4 individual gratin dishes with a leaf, leaving about half of each leaf overhanging the dish. Chop the trimmed stems (about ¼ cup) and reserve. Cut the fish into 4 equal pieces.

Snap the ends of the beans. Place in a microwave-safe container, cover loosely with plastic wrap, and microwave for 30 seconds.

Lay a piece of fish on the chard leaf in each gratin dish. Place a layer of beans over the fish. Top each with 2 tablespoons carrot, 1 tablespoon of the reserved chard stems, 1 tablespoon onion, and ½ tablespoon chervil.

In a small bowl, combine the wine, garlic, and mustard and mix thoroughly. Spoon 2 tablespoons over each gratin. Add salt and pepper.

Fold the overhanging half of the chard leaf over a gratin and, holding it securely folded over, cover the gratin tightly with aluminum foil. Repeat the process for the other 3 gratins and place all on a baking sheet.

Bake for 15 minutes.

YIELD = 4 SERVINGS

Fat per serving = 0.99 g.

Calories per serving = 104.2

Gnocchi Lumache

Blood Orange and Cucumber-Yogurt Salad

⌒

*T*he most labor-intensive step in this menu is cutting the blood oranges for the salad—thanks to the fairly recent arrival of vacuum-packed gnocchi on supermarket shelves! Potato gnocchi have long been among our favorite hearty low-fat foods, but you used to have to make the dumplings from scratch or search out specialty stores that carried fresh pasta. The new vacuum-packed gnocchi are not only terribly convenient, but also tend to hold their shape better than the store-bought fresh variety and to taste more like homemade.

This menu features our rendition of a classic Italian snail (or *lumache*) stew, which is traditionally served on polenta. For variety, omit the gnocchi from the recipe and serve each portion of stew atop 2 broiled or grilled polenta cakes.

99% FAT-FREE FAST STRATEGY:
1. Make and compose the salads.
2. Put a large pot of water up to boil over high heat. While it comes to a boil, drain and chop the ingredients for the gnocchi dish.
3. Start the sauce for the gnocchi in a skillet.
4. Mix the other ingredients into the sauce while the gnocchi cooks in the boiling water.
5. Drain the gnocchi, add to the skillet, and season.

Blood Orange and Cucumber-Yogurt Salad

We use colorful, sweet-tart blood oranges in this recipe, but you can substitute more readily available navel oranges.

10 ounces hothouse cucumber

Four 3½-ounce blood oranges

½ tablespoon chopped fresh mint

¼ cup plain nonfat yogurt

1 tablespoon freshly squeezed orange juice

3 ounces Belgian endive (about 1 head)

Peel and chop the cucumber (about 1 cup). Peel the blood oranges, remove the pith, and cut each into 6 slices with a serrated knife.

In a bowl, combine the cucumber, mint, yogurt, and orange juice. Mix well.

Arrange 4 Belgian endive leaves to form an **X** on each of 4 salad plates. Mound about ¼ cup of the cucumber-yogurt mixture in the center of each, ringed by 6 circles of blood orange.

YIELD = 4 SERVINGS

Fat per serving = 0.22 g.

Calories per serving = 51.0

Gnocchi Lumache

One 7-ounce can snails

One 14½-ounce can diced tomatoes with
    garlic and onion

3 to 4 sprigs fresh flat-leaf parsley

½ cup chopped white onion (precut)

2 teaspoons minced roasted garlic (precut)

2 tablespoons water

1 pound potato gnocchi

One 8-ounce can tomato sauce

Salt and freshly ground black pepper to
    taste

Bring a large pot of water to a boil over high heat. Meanwhile, drain the snails and tomatoes and chop the parsley (about ⅓ cup). In a medium nonstick skillet, combine the onion, garlic, and the 2 tablespoons of water. Cook over high heat for about 1 minute, until the onion is translucent.

Add the gnocchi to the pot of boiling water and cook for about 2½ minutes, until the dumplings rise to the top of the pot. Meanwhile, add the snails, tomatoes, and tomato sauce to the skillet. Stir, reduce the heat to low, and simmer for 2 minutes.

Drain the gnocchi and add them to the mixture in the skillet, along with the parsley, salt, and black pepper.

Serve about 1¼ cups on each of 4 dinner plates.

YIELD = 4 SERVINGS

Fat per serving = 0.65 g.

Calories per serving = 231.4

Don't go back to sorting the mail or reviewing the day's telephone messages while preparing fast-cooking gnocchi, which will be done in 2 to 2½ minutes, as soon as the dumplings rise to the top of the pot.

Smoked Turkey Pinwheels

Potato and Pepper Frittata

Salsa Shrimp Salad

⁓

*T*his menu includes some very versatile dishes. Since the frittata—a kind of omelet—is baked, it holds up well for hours on a buffet table. Here we serve it as a main course, along with a salsa shrimp salad that can also serve as lunch for two (or be doubled to serve four). There's something about the spicy tomato flavor of the salsa that just seems to go naturally with the frittata; think of the combination as a kind of sophisticated, grown-up take on catsup with scrambled eggs. Our turkey pinwheels can also be made in quantity and passed as hors d'oeuvre with cocktails.

The frittata is best allowed to sit for a while after it comes out of the oven. We usually prepare it first; make the other courses while it bakes; and slice it after serving the turkey rolls and then plating the salad.

99% FAT-FREE FAST STRATEGY:
1. Preheat the oven. Meanwhile, prep the onion and roasted peppers for the frittata.
2. While preheating a skillet, combine the frittata ingredients.
3. Remove the skillet from the heat, pour in the mixture, and place in the oven.
4. While the frittata bakes, make and chill the turkey roll.
5. Prep the ingredients for the salad.
6. Mix the salad and place it in the refrigerator, along with the salad plates.
7. Remove the frittata from the oven and set it aside.
8. Cut the turkey roll into pinwheels and serve.
9. Plate the salad atop lettuce leaves on chilled plates. Slice the frittata.

Potato and Pepper Frittata

5 ounces yellow onion (about 1 small onion)

6 ounces sweet roasted peppers (preroasted)

1 cup nonfat liquid egg substitute

2 tablespoons skim milk

8 ounces refrigerated hash brown potatoes (also called shredded potatoes, about 1¼ cups)

Salt and freshly ground black pepper to taste

Preheat the oven to 350 degrees.

Trim the onion, cut it in half lengthwise, and slice thin (about ¾ cup). Drain and thinly slice the roasted peppers (about ½ cup).

Preheat a 10-inch nonstick skillet with an ovenproof handle over high heat.

In a large bowl, whisk the liquid egg substitute and the milk together until frothy. Stir in the onion, roasted peppers, and potatoes. Season with salt and pepper.

Remove the skillet from the heat, pour in the egg mixture, and smooth with a rubber spatula. Bake for 15 to 20 minutes, until the edges are set and the frittata is lightly browned across the top.

Remove from the oven and let sit for about 10 minutes before slicing and serving.

YIELD = 4 SERVINGS

Fat per serving = 0.18 g.

Calories per serving = 91.0

The frittata can also be baked in a well-seasoned cast-iron skillet. If you use cast iron, preheat the skillet in the oven and spray it once lightly with vegetable oil cooking spray.

Smoked Turkey Pinwheels

The flatbread we used in developing this recipe was labeled Armenian bread, but it may also be called "untoasted lavasch," "mountain bread," or "single pita." When selecting a flatbread, look for the thinnest and most pliable rounds. It will be easier to roll up the flatbread if you have the turkey breast sliced very thin at the deli counter.

2 teaspoons honey mustard
One 9-inch round Armenian flatbread
1 leaf red-leaf lettuce

1⅓ ounces hickory-smoked sliced turkey (about 3 slices)
1 ounce bean sprouts (about ¼ cup)

Spread the mustard over the flatbread. Layer with the lettuce leaf and the turkey. Top with the sprouts. Roll up, wrap in plastic wrap, and refrigerate for 10 to 15 minutes.

Cut the roll crosswise into 8 rounds. Serve 2 each as an appetizer.

YIELD = 4 SERVINGS

Fat per serving = 0.74 g.
Calories per serving = 60.6

Salsa Shrimp Salad

1 pound Italian plum tomatoes (about 4 tomatoes)

3 ounces white onion

5 ounces green bell pepper (about 1 small pepper)

6 ounces cooked, peeled medium shrimp

4 ounces fresh cilantro (about 1 bunch)

½ tablespoon chopped jalapeño pepper (precut)

1 teaspoon minced garlic (precut)

¼ cup freshly squeezed lemon juice

Salt and freshly ground black pepper to taste

4 leaves romaine lettuce

Core and quarter the tomatoes. Peel the onion and cut it into 8 equal chunks. Trim and quarter the bell pepper. Cut the shrimp in half crosswise. Chop the cilantro (about ½ cup).

Combine the tomatoes, onion, bell pepper, cilantro, jalapeño pepper, and garlic in a food processor. Pulse 20 to 25 times, until coarsely but uniformly chopped. Transfer to a bowl and mix in the shrimp, lemon juice, and salt and pepper. Refrigerate until ready to serve, at least 10 minutes.

Serve ½ cup salad atop a lettuce leaf on each of 4 chilled salad plates.

YIELD = 4 SERVINGS

Fat per serving = 0.84 g.

Calories per serving = 87.5

Onion Soup

Moroccan Vegetables and Chicken

Cumin Couscous

⁓

*T*hese recipes can take a few minutes more to prepare than most of our menus, but we think it's well worth it. The dishes comprise a very generous meal that is elegant in its rustic simplicity and eminently suitable for entertaining. We've lent a pungent curry accent to the Moroccan-style chicken stew and seasoned the raisin-studded couscous on which it is served with hints of cumin and turmeric, two of the essential components of curry powder.

If you want to serve the onion soup as a first course, don't heat the stock in which the vegetables simmer until you sit down to the soup course.

99% FAT-FREE FAST STRATEGY:

1. Preheat the broiler. Start to prepare the soup.
2. While the soup simmers, prep the vegetables and toast the baguette slices to garnish the soup.
3. Bring the stock for the vegetable and chicken dish to a boil.
4. Add the vegetables to the stock; while it comes back to a boil, make the paste for the chicken.
5. Simmer the vegetables; meanwhile, coat and broil the chicken and bring the stock for the couscous to a boil.
6. Add the remaining ingredients to the couscous. While the couscous steeps, chunk the chicken and add it to the vegetable mixture.
7. Fluff the couscous, serve ¾ cup on each of four dinner plates, and top with 1½ cups of the vegetables and chicken.

Onion Soup

1½ pounds yellow onions (about 3 onions)

¼ cup water

1 teaspoon minced garlic (precut)

½ tablespoon instant beef soup base

¼ cup light corn syrup

¼ cup plus 2 tablespoons dry sherry

4 cups beef stock, skimmed

Four ¼-inch-thick slices French bread

1 teaspoon salt

1 teaspoon dried thyme

Freshly ground black pepper to taste (optional)

2 teaspoons freshly grated Parmesan cheese

Peel and slice the onions (about 3 cups).

Combine the onions and water in a large saucepan and cook over medium-high heat until the liquid starts to steam, 1 to 2 minutes. Cover and cook for about 4 minutes, until the onions are limp and just beginning to brown. Add the garlic and stir just until the mixture begins to give off an aroma, 10 to 15 seconds. Add the soup base and stir a few times, until the onions have darkened a bit. Add the corn syrup and sherry and stir to incorporate. Stir in the beef stock. Bring to a boil, cover, and reduce the heat to maintain a very gentle simmer for 12 minutes.

Meanwhile, toast the French bread lightly.

Stir the seasonings into the soup. Divide the soup among 4 bowls, float a toasted slice of bread in each, and sprinkle with ½ teaspoon Parmesan cheese.

YIELD = 4 SERVINGS

Fat per serving = 0.83 g.

Calories per serving = 208.3

Our rendition of this classic dish is intrinsically so low in fat that you can even top it with a generous sprinkling of grated Parmesan cheese. Toast the slices of French bread that will float atop the soup for about 1 minute per side in the broiler you've preheated for the chicken—or in a toaster oven or a thick-slice toaster.

Moroccan Vegetables and Chicken

3 cups chicken stock (see Pantry)

14 ounces zucchini (2 to 3 zucchini)

9 ounces yellow onions (about 2 onions)

One 14½-ounce can diced tomatoes

One 15½-ounce can butter beans

4 ounces baby-cut carrots (precut)

1 teaspoon curry powder (see Pantry)

¼ teaspoon ground cinnamon

2 teaspoons freshly squeezed lemon juice

6 ounces skinless, boneless chicken breast

Preheat the broiler. Line a broiler pan with aluminum foil.

In a large saucepan, bring the chicken stock to a boil over medium heat. Meanwhile, trim and cut the zucchini into small chunks (about 3 cups) and peel and quarter the onions. Drain the tomatoes and rinse and drain the butter beans.

Add the vegetables to the stock. Bring back to a boil. Meanwhile, combine the curry powder, cinnamon, and lemon juice in a small bowl and mix to form a paste.

Cover the saucepan and simmer the vegetables over medium-low heat until tender, about 10 minutes. While the vegetables simmer, coat the chicken breast on both sides with the paste and transfer it to the prepared pan. Broil for about 4 minutes per side, until brown and crusty.

Remove the chicken from the oven. Cut it into medium-sized chunks and stir it into the vegetable mixture.

YIELD = 4 SERVINGS

Fat per serving = 0.98 g.

Calories per serving = 157.7

Cumin Couscous

1½ cups chicken stock (see Pantry)

¼ teaspoon ground cumin

¼ teaspoon ground turmeric

¼ cup golden raisins

1 cup quick-cooking couscous

In a small saucepan, bring the chicken stock to a boil over high heat. Stir in the remaining ingredients, cover, remove from the heat, and steep for 5 minutes. Stir and fluff with a fork.

YIELD = 4 SERVINGS

Fat per serving = 0.27 g.

Calories per serving = 190.2

Curried Mussels
Portobello Stir-Fry with Mushroom Orzo

~

*T*his is a truly transcultural meal—pairing an Indian curry with a Chinese stir-fry and Italian orzo. Together, these recipes make for a very abundant table. If you wish to serve the mussels as a first course, delay the start of the stir-fry.

99% FAT-FREE FAST STRATEGY:

1. Rinse the mussels under cold running water.
2. Prep the potato and celery for the curry. Meanwhile, preheat a saucepan.
3. Cook the orzo in the hot saucepan. Between additions of stock, prep the bok choy for the stir-fry and preheat a Dutch oven. Remove the orzo from the heat, cover, and set aside.
4. Begin to cook the curry in the hot Dutch oven. Meanwhile, make the sauce for the stir-fry and preheat a wok or skillet.
5. Add the mussels and other remaining ingredients to the curry. While it continues to cook, make the stir-fry in the hot wok or skillet.
6. Mix the finishing ingredients into the orzo.
7. Divide the orzo among four dinner plates and serve alongside about 1¼ cups of the stir-fry.

Curried Mussels

2 pounds debearded mussels (32 to 36 mussels)

6 ounces red potato (about 1 potato)

1 ounce celery (about 1 small stalk)

½ cup canned diced tomatoes

¼ cup plus 2 tablespoons chopped white onion (precut)

1 cup dry white wine or water (or a mixture)

½ tablespoon chopped fresh basil leaves

1 teaspoon curry powder (see Pantry)

Put the mussels in a colander and shake under cold running water for about 1 minute. Discard any mussels that do not close when tapped.

Peel and dice the potato (about ¾ cup) and trim and dice the celery (about 2 tablespoons).

Preheat a Dutch oven over high heat.

Add the potato, celery, tomatoes, onion, and wine and/or water to the hot pot and bring to a boil. Reduce the heat to medium-low, cover, and simmer for about 3 minutes, until the onion is translucent.

Stir in the basil, curry powder, and mussels. Re-cover and cook, shaking the pan periodically, for 5 to 7 minutes more, until the mussels have opened.

Serve 8 to 9 mussels per person.

YIELD = 4 SERVINGS

Fat per serving = 0.97 g.

Calories per serving = 119.7

Look for debearded mussels in the market to save considerable time and effort; they usually come in mesh bags. Like clams, mussels should be put into a colander and held under cold running water; they can die if allowed to sit in fresh water for a prolonged period of time. Discard any mussels with broken shells and those that do not open while cooking.

Mushroom Orzo

Orzo is basically pasta fashioned into tiny granules that resemble grains of rice. In this recipe, we're cooking the orzo as you would a risotto, resulting in a creamier-than-usual consistency.

2 tablespoons water

1 cup sliced white button mushrooms (precut)

½ cup chopped white onion (precut)

2 teaspoons minced garlic (precut)

½ cup orzo

1½ cups chicken stock (see Pantry)

1 tablespoon freshly grated Parmesan cheese

1 tablespoon chopped fresh flat-leaf parsley (optional)

Preheat a medium saucepan over medium heat.

Combine the water, mushrooms, and onion in the hot pan. Cook for about 3 minutes, stirring constantly, until the onion is translucent.

Stir in the garlic and orzo to combine thoroughly, then stir in 1 cup of the chicken stock. Continue to cook, stirring in the remaining stock 2 tablespoons at a time, until the pasta is al dente, about 12 minutes.

Remove from the heat and cover to keep warm until ready to serve. Stir in the Parmesan cheese and, if desired, the parsley.

YIELD = 4 SERVINGS

Fat per serving = 0.89 g.

Calories per serving = 106.5

Portobello Stir-Fry

1¼ pounds bok choy (about 1 head)

¼ cup dry white wine

2 tablespoons Chinese oyster sauce

½ tablespoon reduced–sodium soy sauce

3 tablespoons cornstarch

1½ cups chicken stock (see Pantry)

1 small dried hot pepper

6 ounces sliced portobello mushrooms
(precut; about 16 slices)

1 cup shredded carrots (precut)

Cut the bok choy on the diagonal into thin strips (about 6 cups).

In a bowl, mix together the wine, oyster sauce, soy sauce, cornstarch, and 1 cup of the chicken stock and set aside. Meanwhile, preheat a nonstick wok or a large non-stick skillet over high heat.

Put ¼ cup of the remaining chicken stock and the dried pepper into the hot wok or skillet and cook, stirring constantly, for 1 minute. Add the mushrooms and cook, stirring constantly and turning the mushrooms periodically, until they brown, 1½ to 2 minutes. Remove and reserve the mushrooms.

Add the remaining ¼ cup of chicken stock and the bok choy to the wok or skillet. Stir and add the carrots. Cook and stir for about 1 minute, until the carrots are limp. Add the reserved sauce mixture and stir to coat. Add the reserved mushrooms and any juice they have given off. Continue to cook and stir for another minute or 2, until the sauce thickens and bubbles. Remove the hot pepper before serving.

YIELD = 4 SERVINGS

Fat per serving = 0.50 g.

Calories per serving = 92.1

This recipe showcases wonderful portobello mushrooms, which are meaty enough to satisfy a steak lover!

Egg Drop Soup
Orange Scallop Sauté
Jicama Salad

~

*O*ur refreshing scallop sauté has a strong citrus taste, but is less spicy than the typical orange–flavored Chinese dish. We pair it with a crunchy salad for texture contrast and with a low–fat rendition of classic egg drop soup. Serve the soup while the noodles for the sauté soak and the oven preheats for the salad won tons, then proceed with the rest of the menu.

99% FAT-FREE FAST STRATEGY:
1. Make the soup. While it comes to a boil, set the cellophane noodles aside to soak in hot water, and preheat the oven.
2. Drain the noodles. For the sauté, marinate the scallops, prep the roasted peppers, ginger, garlic, and scallions, and make the sauce.
3. Prep the won ton strips for the salad. While they bake, prep the other salad ingredients.
4. Compose and dress the salad.
5. Preheat a skillet or wok.
6. Make the sauté in the hot skillet. Serve about 1/4 cups on each of 4 dinner plates.

Egg Drop Soup

4 cups chicken stock (see Pantry)

1 cup frozen baby peas

1 cup sliced white button mushrooms
(precut)

½ cup nonfat liquid egg substitute

¼ teaspoon ground white pepper

1 tablespoon chopped fresh cilantro

In a medium saucepan, combine the chicken stock, peas, and mushrooms. Bring to a full boil over medium–high heat, about 4 minutes, and continue to boil for about 1 minute, until the mushrooms are fork tender.

Remove from the heat and add the egg substitute in a thin stream while stirring the soup with a chopstick. Stir in the white pepper and cilantro. Serve 1 cup in each of 4 soup bowls.

YIELD = 4 SERVINGS

Fat per serving = 0.30 g.

Calories per serving = 59.9

We make this egg drop soup with nonfat liquid egg substitute to eliminate superfluous fat; we use flavorful fresh mushrooms instead of the canned mushrooms found in most take–out versions, and finish with a bit of cilantro for added character. Don't thaw the peas; they will be perfectly done and crisp if you add them to the pan while still frozen.

Orange Scallop Sauté

Buy precleaned baby or salad spinach to save the time otherwise required to rinse residual grit from spinach. Baby spinach should need no further prepping; at most you will need to trim the stems of salad spinach.

Cut the ginger into pieces about the size of a quarter.

4 ounces cellophane noodles

1½ cups very hot tap water

3 ounces sweet roasted peppers (preroasted)

1 pound bay scallops

2 tablespoons Triple Sec liqueur

¼ cup reduced-sodium soy sauce

2 tablespoons plus 1 teaspoon cornstarch

2 small pieces fresh ginger

1 clove garlic

2 scallions

1 cup shrimp or vegetable stock (see Pantry)

¼ cup orange juice

One 10-ounce package baby or salad spinach

⅛ teaspoon ground black pepper

1 teaspoon orange zest

In a bowl or measuring cup, combine the cellophane noodles and water and soak the noodles for 10 to 12 minutes, until soft. Drain.

Rinse and drain the roasted peppers. Marinate the scallops in a combination of Triple Sec, 2 tablespoons of the soy sauce, and 1 teaspoon of the cornstarch. Slice the roasted peppers (about ⅓ cup). Peel the ginger and the garlic. Trim and cut the scallions into rings (about ¼ cup). For a sauce, combine the orange juice, the remaining 2 tablespoons of soy sauce and 2 tablespoons of cornstarch, and ¾ cup of the stock.

Preheat a large nonstick skillet or wok over high heat. Combine the remaining ¼ cup of stock, the ginger, and the garlic in the hot pan. Cook, stirring for 1 minute. Add the scallops and marinade and cook for about 2 minutes, stirring, until the scallops are opaque. Remove and discard the ginger and garlic.

Add the spinach and cook and stir for about 30 seconds, just until it's beginning to wilt. Add the cellophane noodles, along with the reserved sauce and sliced roasted peppers. Cook and stir for about 1 minute more, until the spinach is totally wilted. Add the scallions and cook for about 30 seconds, stirring, until the sauce is bubbly. Season with black pepper and orange zest.

YIELD = 4 SERVINGS
Fat per serving = 0.99 g.
Calories per serving = 263.0

Jicama Salad

4 won ton wrappers (also called "dumpling skins," about 1 ounce)

4 ounces jicama

4 ounces fresh snow peas

4 cups cut romaine lettuce

¼ cup pure clover honey

2 teaspoons coarse-grain Dijon mustard

3 tablespoons orange juice

Freshly ground black pepper to taste

Preheat the oven to 350 degrees.

Cut the won ton wrappers into thin strips. Place them on a nonstick baking sheet in a single layer and bake for about 5 minutes, until lightly browned and crispy.

Meanwhile, peel and cut the jicama into matchsticks (about ½ cup). Trim and cut the snow peas on the diagonal into quarters (about ½ cup).

In a large bowl, combine the jicama, snow peas, lettuce, and won ton strips.

Whisk together the honey and mustard in a small bowl. Whisk in the orange juice and add pepper to taste. Pour over the salad and toss to coat.

YIELD = 4 SERVINGS

Fat per serving = 0.33 g.

Calories per serving = 111.5

Baked bits of won tons, which brown nicely without the addition of gobs of butter, are our substitute for typically fatty croutons.

Black Bean Cakes on Salsa

Shrimp and Okra Gumbo

Tomato and Celery Rémoulade

⁓

*T*his menu is our take on a decadent New Orleans repast—but a guilt-less rendition thereof. Our gumbo lacks the typical gobs of fat because we start by making a dry, fat-free roux and use smoked turkey sausage to provide the rich, smoky flavor usually derived from a ham hock. We bake the bean cakes rather than fry them, and strip the rémoulade of fatty mayonnaise.

If you want to serve the bean cakes first, just keep the gumbo warm over low heat and the rémoulade chilled in the refrigerator until ready to serve. Accompanied by only a hunk of bread, the gumbo makes hearty luncheon fare.

99% FAT-FREE FAST STRATEGY:

1. Chill the salad plates; make and refrigerate the rémoulade mixture.
2. Make the bean puree. While it chills, put the rice up to cook. Prep the ingredients for the gumbo, then cook the gumbo vegetables and the flour simultaneously.
3. Mix the cooked flour and other additional ingredients into the vegetables and let the gumbo simmer. Meanwhile, preheat the broiler and form the bean cakes.
4. Add the shrimp to the gumbo; while it finishes cooking, let the rice steep off the heat and broil the bean cakes.
5. Stir the rice into the gumbo. Plate the bean cakes atop the salsa and the rémoulade atop the lettuce leaves.

Tomato and Celery Rémoulade

1½ pounds fresh Italian plum tomatoes
(about 6 tomatoes)

2 ounces scallions (about 3 scallions)

3 ounces celery (about 2 stalks)

1½ tablespoons dry mustard

3 tablespoons freshly squeezed lemon juice

3 tablespoons water

¼ cup plus ½ tablespoon light corn syrup

⅛ teaspoon cayenne pepper

6 leaves romaine lettuce

Put 6 salad plates in the refrigerator to chill.

Core and cut each tomato into 8 chunks. Trim and slice the scallions into rings (about 3 tablespoons). Trim and thinly slice the celery crosswise (about ¾ cup).

In a mixing bowl, combine the mustard, lemon juice, water, corn syrup, and cayenne and whisk thoroughly. Add the tomatoes, scallions, and celery. Toss to coat. Cover and refrigerate until ready to serve.

Lay a lettuce leaf on each of the 6 chilled plates. Divide the rémoulade among the plates and drizzle any residual dressing over the lettuce.

YIELD = 6 SERVINGS

Fat per serving = 0.84 g.

Calories per serving = 78.4

Black Bean Cakes on Salsa

To garnish your bean cakes, be sure to select one of the freshly prepared, high-quality salsas that can be found in refrigerator cases in most markets. Make sure it doesn't contain any oil, which adds superfluous fat grams and actually masks the full flavor of fresh salsa.

Those with particularly incendiary palates can gin up the heat by adding extra hot sauce or choosing a spicy salsa.

One 15½-ounce can black beans

¼ cup nonfat sour cream

1 teaspoon ground cumin

¼ teaspoon salt

1 teaspoon hot sauce

¼ cup yellow cornmeal

¾ cup prepared salsa

Rinse and drain the beans. Transfer them to a food processor, along with the sour cream, seasonings, and 2 tablespoons of the cornmeal. Process to a smooth puree. Scrape into a bowl, cover, and refrigerate for at least 10 minutes.

Preheat the broiler. Line a broiler pan or baking sheet with aluminum foil.

Using ¼ cup of the bean puree for each, form six 3-inch-diameter patties about ½ inch thick. Put the remaining 2 tablespoons of cornmeal onto a plate and coat the top and bottom of of each cake with cornmeal.

Transfer the patties to the prepared pan. Position 2 inches from the heat source and broil for 3 minutes; flip the patties, and broil for about 2 minutes on the other side, until just beginning to brown.

Put 2 tablespoons of the salsa onto each of 6 small plates and top each with a bean cake.

YIELD = 6 SERVINGS

Fat per serving = 0.47 g.

Calories per serving = 99.2

Shrimp and Okra Gumbo

3 cups water

1 cup long-grain white rice

8 ounces red bell pepper (about 1 pepper)

2 ounces celery (about 1 large stalk)

4 ounces smoked turkey sausage

6 ounces cooked, peeled medium shrimp

One 10-ounce package frozen sliced okra,
    thawed

1 cup chopped white onion (precut)

2 teaspoons minced garlic (precut)

1/4 cup all-purpose flour

1 bay leaf

1/2 teaspoon dried thyme

1/4 teaspoon ground black pepper

1/8 teaspoon cayenne pepper

3 1/2 cups chicken stock (see Pantry)

The darker tan the roux becomes while cooking, the richer the gumbo will be—but watch carefully as the flour can burn and blacken quickly.

In a small saucepan, bring 2 1/2 cups of the water to a boil. Stir in the rice, cover, and simmer for 20 minutes. Trim and chop the bell pepper (about 1 cup) and the celery (about 1/2 cup). Chop the sausage (about 1/2 cup). Cut the shrimp in half crosswise.

In a large, heavy-bottomed saucepan or Dutch oven, combine the bell pepper, celery, okra, onion, and garlic. Cook for about 5 minutes over medium heat, stirring occasionally, until the vegetables are limp. Meanwhile, cook the flour in a small cast-iron or other heavy skillet over medium-high heat, stirring constantly, until it turns an even dark tan, about 2 minutes. Remove from the heat. Stir the seasonings into the vegetables. Mix in the cooked flour with a wooden spoon. While stirring, add the chicken stock and the remaining 1/2 cup of water. Bring to a boil, reduce the heat to medium-low, and add the sausage. Cover and simmer for 10 minutes.

Add the shrimp to the gumbo and cook for 5 minutes more. Meanwhile, remove the rice from the heat and set it aside, covered. Remove the bay leaf. Stir in the rice, and ladle 1 1/2 cups into each of 6 soup bowls.

YIELD = 6 SERVINGS

Fat per serving = 0.68 g.

Calories per serving = 201.5

Fisherman's Stew

Couscous Salad

⁓

*T*his is our all-time favorite meal—for company or as a treat to ourselves! By starting with a thick, rich, roasted red pepper puree, we trim the cooking time considerably and preclude the need for cooking raw ingredients in oil. The result is a hearty stew that does not need the usual addition of a slice of bread to thicken it or garlic mayonnaise for flavor. By itself, the broth can also serve as a sauce for pasta or to drizzle over a baked or broiled fish fillet.

We fill the broth with a tasty, low-fat mixture of shellfish and Pacific cod, but the possibilities for creative experimentation are endless. Try adding cracked crab claws, squid rings, red snapper, or tilapia. Serve the salad alongside the stew; the flavors are wonderfully complementary.

99% FAT-FREE FAST STRATEGY:

1. Rinse the clams and mussels under cold running water.
2. Prep the cod and shrimp.
3. Prep the sun-dried tomatoes for the salad: Combine with water, heat in a microwave, add to the dry couscous, and set aside to steep.
4. Make the roasted pepper puree and begin to cook the stew. Mix in the additional ingredients, bring to a boil, and continue to cook.
5. Meanwhile, make the salad dressing.
6. Make final ingredient additions and finish the stew.
7. Fluff and dress the couscous salad; serve atop the lettuce leaves.

Fisherman's Stew

12 ounces littleneck clams (about 8 clams)

8 ounces debearded mussels (about 8 mussels)

6 ounces Pacific cod

4 ounces cooked, peeled medium shrimp

One 12-ounce jar sweet roasted peppers

1 tablespoon minced garlic (precut)

1 teaspoon *fines herbes* (see Pantry)

2 tablespoons drained capers

2 cups clam juice or shrimp stock (see Pantry)

1 cup white wine

2 tablespoons chopped fresh dill

¼ teaspoon hot sauce (or to taste)

Put the clams and mussels in a colander and shake under cold running water for about 1 minute; discard any with broken shells or that do not close when tapped.

Cut the cod into 4 large chunks. Cut the shrimp in half. Rinse and drain the roasted peppers.

Combine the roasted peppers, garlic, *fines herbes,* and 1 tablespoon of the capers in a food processor and puree. Transfer to a Dutch oven and stir in the clam juice or shrimp stock and the wine. Bring to a boil over high heat and boil for 2 minutes. Add the dill, clams, mussels, and the remaining tablespoon of capers. Cover and cook for 5 minutes.

Add the cod and shrimp. Allow the fish to cook through, about 2 minutes, then add the hot sauce. Discard any shellfish that have not opened while cooking and serve.

YIELD = 4 SERVINGS

Fat per serving = 0.64 g.

Calories per serving = 147.3

Couscous Salad

For a cooler, less rich-tasting salad, substitute a cup of diced fresh tomatoes for the sun-dried tomatoes. You could also use our Garlic Spread (page 148) as a dressing in lieu of the Blue Cheese Dressing.

1 ounce sun-dried tomatoes

1 cup water

⅔ cup quick-cooking couscous

½ teaspoon Dijon mustard

¼ cup Blue Cheese Dressing (page 32)

4 leaves romaine lettuce

Chop the sun-dried tomatoes (about ⅓ cup). Combine the tomatoes and water in a microwave-safe container and microwave at full power for 2½ to 3 minutes to bring to a boil.

Put the couscous into a mixing bowl. Pour the boiling water and tomato mixture over it. Stir, cover, and steep for 5 minutes.

Stir the mustard into the blue cheese dressing.

Fluff the couscous with a fork, making sure all the large lumps are broken up. Add the dressing and toss to coat evenly.

Place a leaf of romaine on each of 4 salad plates and serve about ¾ cup of couscous atop each leaf of lettuce.

YIELD = 4 SERVINGS

Fat per serving = 0.86 g. (including dressing)

Calories per serving = 139.2 (including dressing)

Menus
for
Family Meals

Veal with Asparagus, Mushrooms, and Baby Carrots
Garlic Noodle Sauté

⁓

*T*his menu features robust and unique taste combinations. The bourbon boosts the flavor of the veal, enabling us to use a modest enough quantity of meat to stay within our fat ration. The black bean garlic sauce, made from fermented black beans, is savory and aromatic; a little goes a long way. Our noodle sauté is brimming with garlic and chili paste with garlic. Serve the main dish and the noodles side by side; the sauces are complementary, but should be savored separately rather than mixed.

99% FAT-FREE FAST STRATEGY:

1. Put water up to boil for the noodles.
2. While the water comes to a boil, prepare the ingredients and sauce for the veal dish, microwave the carrots, and preheat a skillet or wok.
3. Cook the noodles in the boiling water.
4. While the noodles cook, make the veal dish in the hot skillet or wok. Transfer to a serving dish.
5. Rinse out and reheat the skillet or wok.
6. Drain the noodles and make the sauté.

Garlic Noodle Sauté

6 ounces yolkless broad noodles

½ cup frozen baby peas

3 tablespoons reduced-sodium soy sauce

2 tablespoons water

½ teaspoon minced garlic (precut)

¼ teaspoon chili paste with garlic

Bring a large saucepan of water to a boil over high heat. Add the noodles, stir, and cook for 8 minutes.

Preheat a large nonstick skillet or a nonstick wok over high heat. Drain and add the noodles. Add the remaining ingredients. Cook, stirring constantly, for 1 to 2 minutes, until all the liquid has been absorbed. Serve about 1 cup per person.

YIELD = 4 SERVINGS

Fat per serving = 0.51 g.

Calories per serving = 169.9

Veal with Asparagus, Mushrooms, and Baby Carrots

4 ounces veal scaloppine (top round)

3 tablespoons bourbon

1 tablespoon plus 2 teaspoons cornstarch

8 ounces fresh asparagus (10 to 14 spears)

8 large fresh basil leaves

1¼ cups vegetable stock (see Pantry)

½ tablespoon black bean garlic sauce

1½ cups baby-cut carrots (precut)

2 cups sliced white button mushrooms (precut)

Trim and cut the veal into 2-× ¼-inch strips. In a bowl, mix with the bourbon and 1 tablespoon of the cornstarch and set aside. Trim and cut the asparagus on the diagonal into 3-inch pieces (about 2 cups). Slice the basil leaves (about ¼ cup). For the sauce, combine ¾ cup of the vegetable stock, the remaining 2 teaspoons of cornstarch, and the black bean garlic sauce.

Put the carrots in a microwave-safe container, cover loosely with plastic wrap, and microwave at full power for about 45 seconds, until steaming.

Preheat a large nonstick skillet or a nonstick wok over high heat. Put ¼ cup of the remaining vegetable stock in the hot skillet or wok and heat for 1 minute. Add the mushrooms and asparagus and cook for about 2 minutes, stirring constantly, until the mushrooms begin to brown and the asparagus turns bright green. Add the carrots and cook for 1 minute, stirring, then remove the vegetables to a bowl.

Bring the remaining ¼ cup stock to a boil in the skillet or wok. Add the sauce and cook for about 30 seconds, stirring constantly, until it begins to thicken. Add the veal and cook for about 1 minute, stirring, until the meat is no longer pink. Return the vegetables to the pan and cook and stir for about 1 minute more, until the sauce is thick and bubbly. Stir in the basil. Serve a generous 1 cup per person.

YIELD = 4 SERVINGS

Fat per serving = 0.98 g.

Calories per serving = 109.3

Clam and Mussel Casserole
Asparagus in Black Bean Sauce

⌒

*O*ur shellfish main course is a "big bowl" dish—an updated version of the ever-popular casserole, served up here with Asian undertones echoed in the asparagus with which it is paired. It's an informal menu to be eaten in hands-on style (the clams and mussels are served in the shell, and the asparagus spears are much easier to eat with one's fingers), so you might want to stock some moist towelettes nearby. And don't forget crusty bread for dunking and a bowl for the shells!

The flavorful, but virtually fat-free asparagus—cooked in chicken stock instead of oil—can serve equally well as a first course to a range of seafood entrées.

99% FAT-FREE FAST STRATEGY:
1. Rinse the clams and mussels under cold running water.
2. Prep the leek, mushrooms, garlic, and chard.
3. Make the sauce for the casserole. Meanwhile, preheat a Dutch oven.
4. Cook the leek in the hot pan. Remove from the heat and assemble the remaining layers of the casserole. Return to the stovetop, cover, and cook.
5. Meanwhile, prep, cook, and plate the asparagus dish.
6. Stir the chard into the casserole and finish cooking.

Clam and Mussel Casserole

Be sure to shake the pot periodically while cooking the casserole, to ensure that nothing sticks to the bottom. Discard any clams or mussels that do not open while cooking.

2 pounds littleneck clams (about 24 clams)

1½ pounds debearded mussels (24 to 27 mussels)

6 ounces leek (about 1 leek)

3 ounces fresh shiitake mushrooms (about 6 mushrooms)

4 cloves garlic

2 tablespoons grated fresh ginger (precut)

4 ounces red chard (about 4 leaves)

1 cup chicken stock (see Pantry)

¼ cup dry sherry

2 tablespoons reduced-sodium soy sauce

1 teaspoon sugar

¼ teaspoon chili paste with garlic

2 tablespoons water

2 cups broccoli florets (precut)

Put the clams and mussels in a colander and shake under cold running water for about 1 minute; discard any with broken shells or that do not close when tapped.

Trim the leek to the white part only, cut it in half lengthwise, clean, and slice thin (about ½ cup). Trim, clean, and cut each mushroom into 4 equal strips. Peel and sliver the garlic; combine it in a small bowl with the ginger. Trim and slice the chard (about 2 cups); set it aside.

For the sauce, combine the chicken stock, sherry, soy sauce, sugar, and chili paste in a bowl. Mix and set aside. Preheat a Dutch oven over medium heat.

Combine the leek and water in the hot Dutch oven. Cook for about 2 minutes, until the leek is soft and the water has evaporated. Remove the pot from the heat and place the clams over the leek in a single layer. Cover with half the garlic and ginger mixture, a single layer of mussels, and the remaining garlic and ginger mixture. Top with a layer of mushrooms, a layer of broccoli, and the sauce. Cover and cook over high heat for 8 to 10 minutes, shaking periodically, until the shellfish have opened.

Remove the pan from the heat and stir in the chard. Re-cover, and let sit for 1 minute before serving.

YIELD = 4 SERVINGS

Fat per serving = 0.99 g.

Calories per serving = 103.6

Asparagus in Black Bean Sauce

12 ounces thin asparagus spears (about 32 spears)

4 ounces fresh shiitake mushrooms (about 4 large mushrooms)

½ cup chicken stock (see Pantry)

2 tablespoons black bean garlic sauce

4 leaves romaine lettuce

Trim the asparagus. Trim, clean, and dice the mushrooms (about ¼ cup).

Preheat a nonstick wok or a large nonstick skillet with a lid over high heat.

Add the asparagus and chicken stock to the hot wok or skillet. Cover and cook for about 1 minute, until the asparagus turn bright green. Add the mushrooms and the black bean garlic sauce. Cook for 1 minute more, tossing the asparagus in the sauce to coat.

Place a lettuce leaf on each of 4 salad plates. Divide the asparagus among the prepared plates and drizzle with the residual sauce from the pan.

YIELD = 4 SERVINGS

Fat per serving = 0.69 g.

Calories per serving = 42.1

Cut the mushrooms about the same size as the black beans so that when cooked in the sauce they will cling to the asparagus. We like our asparagus crunchy; cook it for an extra minute before adding the mushrooms and sauce if you prefer yours softer.

Pumpkin Soup
Spicy Turkey Curry
Cumin Basmati Rice

～

*N*ot for those with timid taste buds, this menu brings together a medley of assertive but complementary seasonings. The turkey derives both its bite and its distinctive coloring from Thai red curry paste, which lends the dish a red-orange hue instead of the typical yellow. It plays nicely against the more traditional look and taste of the curried pumpkin soup. The nutty rice has just enough cumin to make it interesting. We like to finish the meal with refreshing Mandarin Orange Sherbet (page 186).

If you want to serve the soup as a first course, delay the start of the actual stir-frying.

99% FAT-FREE FAST STRATEGY:

1. Put the rice up to simmer and proceed with the menu.
2. Make the soup.
3. While the soup cooks, prep the turkey and set it aside to marinate. Prep the remaining ingredients for the curry, make the curry sauce, and microwave the green beans. Keep the soup warm over low heat; garnish with chives just before serving.
4. Preheat a wok or skillet.
5. Put the stock into the hot pan and begin to add and stir-fry the vegetables for the curry. When the vegetables are done, remove them to a bowl.
6. When the rice is done, remove it from the heat and set it aside, covered, to steep.
7. Add the turkey and remaining stock to the wok or skillet and cook. Add the sauce, return the vegetables to the pan, toss to coat, and garnish with the cilantro. Serve about 1¼ cups per person.

Cumin Basmati Rice

1 cup brown basmati rice

2 cups chicken stock (see Pantry)

½ teaspoon ground cumin

In a medium saucepan, combine the rice and chicken stock. Bring to a boil over high heat. Stir in the cumin, cover, and reduce the heat to medium–low. Simmer for 20 to 22 minutes, until the liquid has been absorbed and the rice is tender.

Remove from the heat and set aside, still covered, for about 3 minutes. Fluff with a fork and serve.

YIELD = 4 SERVINGS

Fat per serving = 0.06 g.

Calories per serving = 163.4

For variety, add about ⅓ cup chopped sun–dried tomatoes to the pot, along with the rice and stock.

Pumpkin Soup

Even though this soup, which entails almost no work, starts with canned pumpkin, it's so thick and robust that it tastes as if it were made from scratch.

One 15-ounce can pure pumpkin

2 cups chicken stock (see Pantry)

½ cup skim milk

1 teaspoon curry powder (see Pantry)

Salt and freshly ground black pepper to taste

Snipped fresh chives for garnish

In a medium saucepan, combine the pumpkin and chicken stock. Whisk to blend, then whisk in the skim milk and curry powder. Cook over medium heat for about 10 minutes, until steaming, taking care not to boil. Season with salt and pepper.

Keep warm over low heat until ready to serve. Ladle 1 cup into each of 4 soup bowls and garnish with the chives.

YIELD = 4 SERVINGS

Fat per serving = 0.23 g.

Calories per serving = 43.3

Spicy Turkey Curry

10 ounces turkey breast tenderloin

1 tablespoon plus 2 teaspoons cornstarch

3 tablespoons Thai fish sauce

1 tablespoon freshly squeezed lemon juice

4 ounces yellow onion (about 1 small onion)

6 ounces red bell pepper (about 1 pepper)

4 ounces green beans (about 24 beans)

2 pieces fresh ginger (each about the size of a quarter)

1 clove garlic

2 ounces fresh cilantro

1 tablespoon red curry paste

1¼ cups plus 2 tablespoons chicken stock (see Pantry)

½ cup canned sliced bamboo shoots, rinsed and drained

The trick to this and other stir-fries is to cut all the ingredients into pieces of about the same size to promote even cooking. Longer-cooking ingredients, such as the green beans in this recipe or the broccoli in the Thai Chicken with Water Chestnuts and Broccoli (page 120) are precooked a bit before the stir-fry is started. Assemble all the ingredients by the side of your wok so that you will be able to work quickly once you begin.

Trim and cut the turkey into thin strips. Combine in a bowl with 1 tablespoon of the cornstarch, 2 tablespoons of the fish sauce, and the lemon juice. Mix and set aside.

Peel and cut the onion into thin wedges (about 1 cup). Trim and slice the bell pepper into long strips (about 1 cup). Trim the green beans. Peel the ginger and the garlic. Chop the cilantro (about ¼ cup).

For the curry sauce, combine the remaining 2 teaspoons of cornstarch, the remaining tablespoon of fish sauce, the curry paste, and 1 cup of the chicken stock in a small bowl.

Put the green beans into a microwave-safe container, cover loosely with plastic wrap, and microwave at full power until steaming, about 1 minute. Leave wrapped until ready to use.

Preheat a nonstick wok or a large nonstick skillet over high heat. Combine ¼ cup of the remaining chicken stock, the ginger, and the garlic in the hot wok or skillet. Cook and stir for 30 seconds. Add the onion, bell pepper, and bamboo shoots. Cook for about 2 minutes, stirring constantly, until the onion is translucent. Add the green beans. Cook for about 1 minute more, stirring, until the bamboo

shoots have just begun to brown. Discard the ginger and garlic and transfer the contents of the pan to a bowl.

Combine the remaining 2 tablespoons of chicken stock and the turkey in the wok or skillet. Cook for about 2 minutes, stirring constantly, until the meat is no longer pink. Add the prepared curry sauce and cook and stir for about 1 minute more, until the sauce is thick and bubbly. Return the vegetables to the pan and toss to coat.

Garnish with the cilantro and serve about 1¼ cups per person.

YIELD = 4 SERVINGS

Fat per serving = 0.97 g.

Calories per serving = 137.1

Chicken Scaloppine with Polenta
White Bean Garlic Salad

⌒

*T*his cold weather meal pairs a hearty chicken stew served atop polenta cakes with a very garlicky salad. Serve the salad as a first course or alongside the chicken. Unlike the dish you may remember from childhood, our scaloppine is not dredged to death in flour; the sauce, an intense but delicate bourbon and mushroom mixture, is much more robust than the typical wine sauce. Those willing to splurge a bit on fat counts could substitute veal scaloppine for the chicken.

If you wish to make your own polenta, follow the directions on page 18, adding ¼ cup chopped wild mushrooms instead of the garlic or chives.

99% FAT-FREE FAST STRATEGY:
1. Make and dress the salad.
2. While preheating the oven, make the mushroom dressing for the stew and prep the reserved mushrooms.
3. Slice and bake the polenta on one side. Meanwhile, prep the chicken and microwave the broccoli.
4. While the polenta bakes on the second side, preheat a skillet and stir-fry the chicken, mushrooms, and broccoli in the dressing.
5. Mix in the remaining ingredients and finish cooking the stew.
6. Place two polenta cakes in each of four shallow bowls and top them with about ¾ cup of the chicken mixture.

White Bean Garlic Salad

7 ounces escarole

1 scallion

3 ounces sweet roasted peppers
(preroasted)

One 15-ounce can navy beans

1 tablespoon minced roasted garlic (precut)

½ tablespoon chopped fresh oregano

1 teaspoon Dijon mustard

1 tablespoon freshly squeezed lemon juice

Trim and roughly tear the escarole (about 2 cups). Trim and chop the scallion (about 1 tablespoon plus 1 teaspoon). Rinse, drain, and dice the roasted peppers (about ⅓ cup). Rinse and drain the beans.

Combine the beans, roasted peppers, scallion, garlic, and oregano in a bowl.

In a small bowl, whisk together the mustard and lemon juice. Pour the dressing over the bean mixture and toss to coat.

Put ½ cup escarole on each of 4 salad plates. Top with about ½ cup of the bean mixture.

YIELD = 4 SERVINGS

Fat per serving = 0.72 g.

Calories per serving = 130.0

Chicken Scaloppine with Polenta

1 cup Mushroom Dressing plus reserved mushrooms (page 48)

12 ounces polenta with wild mushrooms (see menu headnote)

6 ounces chicken scaloppine

2 cups broccoli florets (precut)

½ teaspoon minced garlic (precut)

¼ teaspoon cornstarch

Salt and freshly ground black pepper to taste

Look for chicken scaloppine at the butcher shop or supermarket; it's chicken breast that has been butterflied and pounded thin.

Preheat the oven to 400 degrees. Stem and slice the mushrooms reserved from preparation of the dressing (about ½ cup).

Cut the polenta into eight ½-inch-thick slices. Place on a nonstick cookie or baking sheet and bake for 5 minutes. Meanwhile, cut the chicken scaloppine in half lengthwise, then cut it crosswise into ½-inch-thick strips (about ⅔ cup). Put the broccoli into a microwave-safe container, cover loosely with plastic wrap, and microwave for about 1 minute, until bright green and steaming.

Flip the slices of polenta and bake for about 5 minutes more, until lightly browned. Meanwhile, preheat a medium nonstick skillet over high heat. Add 2 tablespoons of the mushroom dressing, the reserved mushrooms, the chicken, and the broccoli. Cook for 2 minutes, stirring constantly. Mix the cornstarch into the remaining dressing and pour it over the contents of the skillet. Cook and stir just until bubbly. Season with salt and pepper.

For each serving, top 2 polenta cakes with ¾ cup of the scaloppine.

YIELD = 4 SERVINGS

Fat per serving = 0.77 g.

Calories per serving = 227.1

Lasagna

Arugula Salad

Tomato Bread

⁓

$\mathcal{O}$ur quick, light rendition of usually long-baked and heavily-sauced lasagna is an easy one-pot meal. It's perfect for those times when you want an old-fashioned, comfort food type of dinner—but don't have the time, energy, or inclination to make it the old-fashioned way. The combination of chicken, aniseed, and *fines herbes* approximates the taste of sausage with none of the fat. If you prefer a meatless lasagna, simply eliminate the chicken and aniseed from the recipe.

99% FAT-FREE FAST STRATEGY:

1. Put water up to boil for the noodles and start the sauce for the lasagna. Meanwhile, prep the chicken.
2. Mix the additional ingredients into the sauce.
3. Break the noodles into the boiling water. While both the sauce and the noodles cook, make the salad and preheat the broiler.
4. Toast the bread on one side, remove it from the broiler, and top.
5. Drain the noodles, toss with the sauce, and make the final ingredient additions. While the lasagna finishes cooking, broil the tomato bread.
6. Divide the lasagna among six shallow bowls and place a slice of tomato bread on the side of each salad plate.

Lasagna

6 ounces white onion (about 1 onion)

8 ounces green bell pepper
(about 1 pepper)

2 tablespoons water

4 ounces skinless, boneless chicken breast

Two 14½-ounce cans diced tomatoes

1 tablespoon *fines herbes* (see Pantry)

¼ teaspoon aniseed

⅛ teaspoon crushed red pepper

8 ounces lasagna noodles

Salt to taste

1 cup skim milk ricotta cheese

Bring a large pot of water to a boil over high heat. Peel the onion, cut it in half lengthwise, and slice thin (about 1 cup). Trim the bell pepper, cut it in half crosswise, and slice thin (about 1 cup).

Combine the onion, bell pepper, and 2 tablespoons of water in a large nonstick skillet. Cook over medium-low heat for 5 to 6 minutes, until the vegetables are soft (the onion will have turned translucent).

While the vegetables cook, cut the chicken into chunks and put it into a food processor. Process for about 1 minute, until finely ground. Add the ground chicken to the skillet with the vegetables and cook for 1 to 2 minutes, stirring constantly, until the meat is no longer pink. Add the tomatoes and stir to incorporate. Stir in the *fines herbes,* aniseed, and crushed pepper. Continue to cook the sauce over medium-low heat, uncovered, for about 15 minutes more, until thick.

Meanwhile, break the lasagna noodles into bite-sized pieces and add to the boiling water. Cook over high heat to desired tenderness, about 12 minutes, and drain.

Add the drained pasta to the skillet and toss to coat. Add salt. Dollop the ricotta cheese over the top. Cover and cook over very low heat for 1 minute.

YIELD = 6 SERVINGS

Fat per serving = 0.85 g.

Calories per serving = 220.9

Avoid preground chicken; by chopping the meat yourself in a food processor, you can control the amount of fat. Nutritional counts vary greatly for lasagna noodles; select a product that has no more than 0.5 grams of fat for every 2 ounces, or substitute yolkless broad noodles.

Arugula Salad

The sweet and sour dressing for this salad provides a nice foil for the spicy taste of the arugula.

12 ounces arugula (about 2 bunches)

¼ cup pure clover honey

1 tablespoon Dijon mustard

2 tablespoons balsamic vinegar

Stem the arugula, cut it into bite-sized pieces (about 6 cups), and place in a large bowl.

Whisk the mustard and honey together in a small bowl, then whisk in the vinegar until well blended. Pour over the arugula and toss to coat.

YIELD = 6 SERVINGS

Fat per serving = 0.34 g.

Calories per serving = 56.7

Tomato Bread

Six ½-inch-thick slices French bread

6 ounces fresh Italian plum tomatoes
(about 1½ tomatoes)

¾ teaspoon minced garlic (precut)

½ tablespoon freshly grated Parmesan
cheese

Preheat the broiler. Core and cut the tomatoes lengthwise into 6 slices.

Lay the bread on a broiler tray and toast on 1 side in the broiler. Turn the slices over, top each with a slice of tomato, and sprinkle with the minced garlic and Parmesan cheese. Return to the broiler until the bread has toasted and the cheese has begun to melt, taking care not to let it brown.

YIELD = 6 SERVINGS

Fat per serving = 0.26 g.

Calories per serving = 51.9

Sometimes we whip up a supply of tomato bread to serve by itself as an hors d'oeuvre; the recipe can be doubled easily.

Hot and Sour Soup
Broccoli, Shiitake, and Chicken Stir-Fry
Chinese Rice

~

*C*hinese food—of the takeout variety—has received some bad press because of its often high-fat content. This menu is our attempt to show how healthful the cuisine actually is when properly prepared.

If you want to serve the hot and sour soup as a first course, delay the start of the actual stir-frying until afterward. The soup can also serve as a meal for four all by itself.

99% FAT-FREE FAST STRATEGY:

1. Put the rice up to cook. Meanwhile, soak the dried mushrooms and wood ears for the soup and prep the broccoli, mushrooms, and chicken for the stir-fry.
2. While bringing the stock to a boil for the soup, prep the reconstituted mushrooms and wood ears.
3. Proceed to make the soup. Keep it warm over low heat.
4. Make the rice. Remove it from the heat and cover to keep warm.
5. Preheat a wok or skillet. Meanwhile, combine the ingredients for the stir-fry sauce.
6. Make the stir-fry in the hot wok or skillet.
7. Divide the soup among six soup bowls, and garnish. Serve the rice and the stir-fry family style in large bowls.

Chinese Rice

2 cups plus 3 tablespoons water

1 cup long—grain white rice

1 tablespoon reduced—sodium soy sauce

1 tablespoon dry sherry

1 tablespoon rice wine vinegar

1 cup frozen baby peas

Bring 2 cups of the water to a boil in a medium saucepan. Stir in the rice, reduce the heat to low, cover, and simmer for 15 minutes.

In a large nonstick skillet, combine the soy sauce, sherry, vinegar, peas, and the remaining 3 tablespoons of water and cook over medium—high heat. When the mixture begins to steam, add the rice and toss to coat it. Cook for 2 to 3 minutes more, until all the liquid has been absorbed. Remove from the heat and cover to keep warm.

YIELD = 6 SERVINGS

Fat per serving = 0.13 g.

Calories per serving = 121.5

Think of this dish as fried rice that's not really fried, since we use no oil. (Because we add the soy sauce, sherry, and vinegar to the cooked rice as soon as we start to "fry" it, there's no need to use oil as a cooking liquid.)

When you do indulge in Chinese takeout food, freeze the always—too—abundant portions of white rice that accompany the order— eliminating the need to cook rice from scratch for future meals. If you start this dish with precooked rice, use 3 cups.

Hot and Sour Soup

In this abundant soup, we've increased the normal ration of vegetables and done away with the fatty pork and tofu. If your market doesn't stock dried shiitakes and wood ears, look in an Asian grocery.

2 ounces dried shiitake mushrooms (also called "black Chinese mushrooms"; 12 to 14 mushrooms)

¼ cup dried wood ears (also called "black fungus")

1 cup very hot tap water

6 cups chicken stock (see Pantry)

2 tablespoons reduced-sodium soy sauce

3 tablespoons distilled white vinegar

1 tablespoon grated ginger (precut)

¾ teaspoon ground black pepper

½ cup frozen baby peas

¾ cup frozen corn kernels

3 tablespoons cornstarch

¼ cup plus 2 tablespoons cool water

2 scallions

Combine the dried mushrooms and wood ears in a bowl, add the hot water, cover, and set aside to soak for 8 to 10 minutes, until soft.

In a large saucepan, bring the chicken stock to a boil over medium-high heat. Meanwhile, squeeze any excess water from the mushrooms and wood ears, then stem and thinly slice the mushrooms.

Add the soy sauce, vinegar, ginger, and pepper to the boiling stock and stir to blend. Stir in the peas, corn, mushrooms, and wood ears. Reduce the heat to medium and cook for 3 minutes. Meanwhile, mix the cornstarch and the cool water and trim and slice the scallions into thin rings.

Stir the cornstarch and water mixture into the soup and cook for 1 to 2 minutes more, until the soup has thickened. Keep warm over low heat until ready to serve. Garnish with the scallion rings.

YIELD = 6 SERVINGS

Fat per serving = 0.28 g.
Calories per serving = 88.6

Broccoli, Shiitake, and Chicken Stir-Fry

8 ounces Chinese broccoli or broccoli raab

4 ounces fresh shiitake mushrooms (about 8 mushrooms)

8 ounces skinless, boneless chicken breast

¼ cup Chinese oyster sauce

2 tablespoons dry sherry

½ teaspoon sugar

1 tablespoon reduced–sodium soy sauce

¼ cup water

1 teaspoon minced garlic (precut)

1 teaspoon grated ginger (precut)

Trim and cut the broccoli into 2–inch pieces (about 2 cups) and trim, clean, and halve the mushrooms (about 1 generous cup). Cut the chicken into strips 2 inches long and about ⅛ inch wide.

Preheat a nonstick wok or a large nonstick skillet over medium heat. Meanwhile, combine the oyster sauce, sherry, and sugar in a bowl. Stir and set aside.

Add the chicken and soy sauce to the hot wok or skillet. Cook for about 1 minute, stirring constantly, until the chicken is no longer pink and the soy sauce has been absorbed. Transfer the chicken to a plate.

Add the broccoli and water to the wok or skillet. Cook the broccoli over medium–high heat for about 2 minutes, stirring constantly, until it turns bright green. Add the garlic and ginger and cook, stirring, for 1 minute. Add the mushrooms and continue to cook and stir for about 20 seconds, until the mushrooms are heated through and all the liquid has been absorbed.

Return the chicken to the pan, add the reserved oyster sauce mixture, and cook and stir for about 20 seconds more to coat and heat.

YIELD = 6 SERVINGS

Fat per serving = 0.71 g.

Calories per serving = 85.3

Chinese broccoli is quite a bit more flavorful than the domestic variety, but it's seasonal and usually to be found only in Asian groceries. Enjoy it when you can; otherwise substitute broccoli raab (rapini). Because of the robust flavor combination of Chinese broccoli or broccoli raab and oyster sauce, we easily omit the sesame oil typically used in stir–fries.

Mediterranean Pasta

Three-Legume Salad

—

*Y*ou'll hardly recognize our modern rendition of this age–old family meal! The *fines herbes* lend a Mediterranean accent to the pasta dish which is really a svelte tuna casserole for the new millennium. We've replaced the canned mushroom soup, frozen peas, and elbow macaroni of your mother's recipe with a light sauce, fresh mushrooms, and yolkless noodles, and dispensed with the once–requisite crust of crushed potato chips.

Our sophisticated version of three–bean salad retires kidney beans, string beans, and wax beans in favor of black beans, navy beans, and pinto beans, to which we add a fresh balsamic and Dijon dressing in lieu of the traditional ration of bottled, oil–based dressing.

99% FAT–FREE FAST STRATEGY:

1. Put water up to boil for the noodles. While it comes to a boil, prep the roasted peppers and tomatoes for the salad.
2. Cook the noodles in the boiling water. Meanwhile, make and dress the salad.
3. Drain the noodles.
4. Preheat a skillet.
5. Start to cook the pasta mixture in the hot skillet. While it cooks, drain the tuna and combine the milk and flour.
6. Mix the additional ingredients into the pasta and finish cooking.

Mediterranean Pasta

6 ounces yolkless fine noodles

1 cup sliced white button mushrooms (precut)

1 cup chopped white onion (precut)

2 cups broccoli florets (precut)

¼ cup water

One 6-ounce can light tuna in water

1 tablespoon flour

1 cup skim milk

½ tablespoon *fines herbes* (see Pantry)

Salt and freshly ground black pepper to taste

*T*una varies in fat content; compare nutritional labels and be sure to choose a variety packed in water rather than oil. If you feel particularly indulgent, add a light sprinkling of freshly grated Parmesan cheese.

Bring a large saucepan of water to a boil.

Add the noodles to the boiling water and cook over medium-high heat for about 4 minutes, until tender. Drain and set aside.

Preheat a large nonstick skillet over medium-high heat.

Combine the mushrooms, onion, broccoli, and ¼ cup water in the hot skillet. Stir, cover, and cook for about 3 minutes, until the water has evaporated, the onion is translucent, and the broccoli is bright green. Meanwhile, drain the tuna and mix the flour into the skim milk.

Stir the milk and flour mixture and the *fines herbes* into the skillet. Stir in the tuna. Add the noodles to the skillet and toss to mix well. Cook for 30 to 60 seconds more, until the liquid has been absorbed and the mixture is steamy. Season with salt and pepper.

Serve a generous 1¼ cups per person.

YIELD = 4 SERVINGS

Fat per serving = 0.94 g.

Calories per serving = 260.9

Three-Legume Salad

¾ cup canned black beans

¾ cup canned navy beans

½ cup canned pinto beans

6 ounces sweet roasted peppers
(preroasted)

8 ounces fresh Italian plum tomatoes
(about 2 tomatoes)

¼ cup light corn syrup

2 tablespoons red wine vinegar

1 tablespoon balsamic vinegar

2 teaspoons Dijon mustard

½ tablespoon *fines herbes* (see Pantry)

½ teaspoon salt

¼ teaspoon ground black pepper

2 cups cut romaine lettuce

Rinse and drain the black beans, navy beans, and pinto beans. Rinse, drain, and chop the roasted peppers (about ⅔ cup). Core and chop the tomatoes (about 1 cup). Combine the beans, roasted peppers, and tomatoes in a bowl and mix.

For the dressing, combine the remaining ingredients (except the lettuce) in a small bowl and whisk thoroughly. Pour over the salad and mix to coat.

Put ½ cup of the lettuce on each of 4 plates and top with about ¾ cup of the salad.

YIELD = 4 SERVINGS

Fat per serving = 0.91 g.

Calories per serving = 192.1

Mexican Lasagna
Spicy Shrimp and Melon Salad

⁓

*T*his is a fabulous quick family meal. On the odd chance you have any leftover lasagna, serve it up for lunch; this is one of those classic casseroles that are even better the next day. The lasagna is layered with the virtually fat-free flour tortillas that recently landed in supermarket refrigerator cases; they are exactly 9 inches and fit perfectly into a cake pan. We like the complexity of three layers, but you could just as easily put all the meat in one layer.

Make the elegant salad, which provides an interesting contrast to the down-home casserole, while the lasagna is baking, and serve the dishes simultaneously. Like the lasagna, the salad contains a generous dose of zippy chili powder.

99% FAT-FREE FAST STRATEGY:

1. Preheat the oven. Meanwhile, chop the turkey in a food processor and make the ricotta cheese mixture.
2. Preheat a skillet. Cook the turkey and onion in the hot skillet. Mix in the additional ingredients, simmer, and remove from the heat.
3. Layer the lasagna in a cake pan, cover, and put in the oven.
4. While the lasagna bakes, prepare the shrimp, lettuce, and cantaloupe components of the salad.
5. Uncover the lasagna, sprinkle with the cheese, and return it to the oven to finish baking. Allow it to cool briefly before slicing.
6. Plate the salad.

Mexican Lasagna

For a more traditional Mexican look, sprinkle nonfat cheddar cheese over the top in lieu of the mozzarella. The lasagna is easiest to cut with a serrated knife.

6 ounces turkey breast tenderloin

One 14½-ounce can diced tomatoes with basil, garlic, and oregano

¾ cup skim milk ricotta cheese

⅓ cup plus 2 tablespoons shredded nonfat mozzarella cheese

2 tablespoons nonfat liquid egg substitute

2 tablespoons chopped fresh cilantro

Salt and freshly ground black pepper to taste

½ cup chopped white onion (precut)

1 teaspoon minced roasted garlic (precut)

½ tablespoon chili powder

Four 9-inch nonfat flour tortillas

Preheat the oven to 400 degrees. Chop the turkey in a food processor (about ⅔ cup). Drain the tomatoes. In a bowl, mix together the ricotta cheese, ⅓ cup of the mozzarella cheese, the egg substitute, cilantro, and salt and pepper.

Preheat a medium nonstick skillet over high heat. Add the turkey and onion to the skillet. Cook for about 2 minutes, until the turkey is no longer pink and has begun to brown. Reduce the heat to medium and add the tomatoes, garlic, and chili powder. Simmer for about 2 minutes, until the sauce has thickened. Add salt and pepper. Remove from the heat and set aside.

Line a nonstick 9-inch round cake pan with 1 of the tortillas. Spread 1 cup of the turkey mixture over the tortilla, leaving a 1-inch border. Place a second tortilla on top and spread with all of the ricotta mixture, again leaving a 1-inch border. Add a third tortilla and cover to within an inch of the outside with the remaining turkey mixture. Top with the fourth tortilla and cover with aluminum foil.

Bake for 10 minutes, then remove the foil and scatter the remaining 2 tablespoons of mozzarella cheese over the top of the casserole. Bake for about 2 minutes more, until the cheese melts and the tortilla browns.

Remove from the oven and allow to sit for 2 minutes before cutting.

YIELD = 4 SERVINGS

Fat per serving = 0.95 g.

Calories per serving = 245.6

Spicy Shrimp and Melon Salad

4 ounces fresh cilantro

¼ cup dry vermouth

1 tablespoon pure clover honey

½ teaspoon minced roasted garlic (precut)

2 teaspoons chili powder

½ teaspoon salt

¼ cup freshly squeezed lime juice

6 ounces cooked, shelled medium shrimp

4 cups cut romaine lettuce

2 tablespoons chopped fresh mint

2 teaspoons sugar

12 ounces cantaloupe cubes (precut, about 2 cups)

Look for precut melon in the produce section or on the salad bar at your local market.

Chop the cilantro (about ½ cup). In a bowl, combine the cilantro, vermouth, honey, garlic, chili powder, salt, and 2 tablespoons of the lime juice. Remove 2 tablespoons of the mixture to a small bowl, add the shrimp, and toss to coat. Toss the lettuce in the remaining dressing.

In a second small bowl, mix together the mint, sugar, and remaining 2 tablespoons of lime juice. Add the cantaloupe and mix well.

Put 1 cup of the lettuce on each of 4 salad plates. Add ½ cup of the cantaloupe, and top with 2 tablespoons of the shrimp.

YIELD = 4 SERVINGS

Fat per serving = 0.96 g.

Calories per serving = 109.3

Chicken Cacciatore

Spinach Salad

⌒

*I*n this menu, we pair hearty chicken cacciatore, or Italian "hunter's stew," with a cold spinach salad in a sweet and sour dressing that tastes like the high-fat version usually used to dress hot spinach salads.

Cutting the chicken into cubes instead of making the stew with quartered chicken eliminates the need to prebrown the meat in oil, saving both time and fat grams—and allowing for abundant portions. Omit the chicken for a virtually fat-free vegetarian dish that can be served on noodles or rice and that is also quite good as a sauce for baked cod, in lieu of our Tomato Basil Salsa (page 29).

99% FAT-FREE FAST STRATEGY:

1. Prep the bell pepper and chicken. Preheat a skillet.
2. Start the chicken cacciatore in the hot skillet.
3. Mix in the additional ingredients, bring to a boil, and allow to simmer.
4. Meanwhile, make and dress the salad. Preheat the broiler.
5. Slice and broil the polenta.
6. Finish cooking the chicken cacciatore.
7. Place 2 slices of polenta in each of four shallow bowls and top with about one cup of the stew.

Chicken Cacciatore

8 ounces green bell pepper (about 1 pepper)

6 ounces skinless, boneless chicken breast

One 14½-ounce can diced tomatoes with basil, garlic, and oregano

1 cup chopped white onion (precut)

2 tablespoons water

1⅓ cups sliced white button mushrooms (precut)

½ teaspoon minced fresh garlic (precut)

One 8-ounce can tomato sauce

1 bay leaf

⅛ teaspoon ground black pepper

½ teaspoon salt

¼ teaspoon celery seed

12 ounces polenta (see Pantry)

¼ cup dry red wine

Trim, seed, and dice the bell pepper (about 1 cup). Cut the chicken into ¾-inch cubes. Drain the tomatoes.

Preheat a large skillet over medium-high heat.

Combine the onion, bell pepper, and water in the hot skillet and sauté for about 3 minutes, until the onion is translucent. Add the mushrooms and garlic and cook for 1 minute. Stir in the chicken. Cook, stirring constantly, until the meat is no longer pink, 1 to 2 minutes more. Stir in the tomatoes, tomato sauce, bay leaf, black pepper, salt, and celery seed. Bring to a boil, cover, reduce the heat to medium-low, and simmer for 20 minutes.

Meanwhile, preheat the broiler. Cut the polenta into eight ½-inch-thick slices and place them on a broiler tray lined with aluminum foil. Broil the polenta cakes for about 2 minutes per side, until lightly browned.

When the chicken has simmered, uncover the skillet, remove the bay leaf, and add the wine. Raise the heat to high and boil for 2 minutes.

For each serving, top 2 slices of polenta with 1 cup of the stew.

YIELD = 4 SERVINGS

Fat per serving = 0.92 g.

Calories per serving = 198.5

Since we use one of the new varieties of preseasoned canned tomatoes in this dish, there's no need to extend cooking time precious extra minutes to allow for the seasonings to be absorbed. This recipe also lends itself to the use of frozen precut bell peppers; if you use frozen instead of fresh, eliminate the 2 tablespoons of water.

Spinach Salad

Our Dijon mustard and balsamic vinegar mixture has the sweet and sour taste of the classic warm spinach dressing, but none of the bacon fat. Thinly sliced apples, which blend wonderfully with the brown sugar in the dressing, add color and a bit of crunch, as well as flavor.

4 ounces red onion

7 ounces firm, tart red apple (about 1 apple)

2 teaspoons Dijon mustard

2 tablespoons balsamic vinegar

2 tablespoons packed dark brown sugar

3 ounces baby spinach (about 1½ cups)

Freshly ground black pepper to taste

Peel the onion and slice thin (about ¾ cup). Core the apple and slice very thin (about 1⅓ cups.)

For the dressing, in a small bowl, combine the mustard, vinegar, and brown sugar and mix well.

Combine the spinach, onion, and apple in a bowl. Add the dressing and black pepper. Toss to mix and coat thoroughly. Divide among 4 salad plates.

YIELD = 4 SERVINGS

Fat per serving = 0.39 g.

Calories per serving = 63.5

Pad Thai
Thai Salad

⌒

*W*e like to serve these dishes simultaneously, family style, on big platters, along with extra bean sprouts, lime wedges, and some spicy Thai chili sauce that can be mixed in by each person according to taste. The Pad Thai is basically a sweet and sour noodle dish, made with rice stick vermicelli and Thai fish sauce, both of which can be found in the Asian section of most supermarkets.

99% FAT-FREE FAST STRATEGY:
1. Bring water to a boil for the vermicelli.
2. While the vermicelli steeps, make the salad dressing and the salad and prep the scallions, shrimp, and cilantro.
3. Preheat a skillet. Meanwhile, combine the vinegar mixture.
4. Drain and cook the vermicelli in the vinegar mixture in the hot skillet. Add the remaining ingredients and finish the dish.
5. Dress the salad.

Pad Thai

Because we use no oil in this recipe, the noodles may be less crisp than some might expect.

4 cups water

8 ounces rice stick vermicelli

2 ounces scallions (about 3 scallions)

5 ounces cooked, peeled medium shrimp

2 ounces fresh cilantro

1/4 cup plus 2 tablespoons rice wine vinegar

1/4 cup plus 2 tablespoons sugar

1/4 cup Thai fish sauce

1/4 teaspoon cayenne pepper

8 ounces mung bean sprouts (about 2 cups)

1 lime

In a medium saucepan, bring the water to a boil over high heat. Add the vermicelli. Bring back to a boil, cover, and set aside off the heat for 12 minutes, until soft.

Trim and slice the scallions on the diagonal (about 1/3 cup). Cut the shrimp in half crosswise. Chop the cilantro (about 1/4 cup).

Preheat a medium nonstick skillet over medium heat. Meanwhile, in a bowl, combine the vinegar, sugar, fish sauce, and cayenne, and mix.

Drain the vermicelli and add it to the hot skillet, along with the vinegar mixture. Cook, stirring constantly, for about 3 minutes, until all the liquid has been absorbed. Stir in the scallions, sprouts, and shrimp. Cook for 1 minute more to heat through.

Cut the lime into wedges. Garnish with the cilantro and lime wedges.

YIELD = 4 SERVINGS

Fat per serving = 0.66 g.

Calories per serving = 348.7

Thai Salad

¼ cup boiling water

¼ cup plus 2 tablespoons sugar

¼ teaspoon salt

¼ cup plus 2 tablespoons white wine
vinegar

½ teaspoon chili paste with garlic

4 ounces carrot (about 1 carrot)

7 ounces tomato (about 1 tomato)

2 ounces watercress

4 cups cut romaine lettuce

In a bowl, combine the boiling water, sugar, and salt and mix to dissolve the sugar.
Whisk in the vinegar and chili paste. Cover and refrigerate until ready to use.

Peel and slice the carrot on the diagonal (about ½ cup). Core and cut the tomato
into 16 wedges. Remove the thick stems from the watercress (about ½ cup). In a bowl,
combine the carrot, lettuce, tomato, and watercress.

Dress the salad and toss to coat.

YIELD = 4 SERVINGS

Fat per serving = 0.37 g.

Calories per serving = 62.0

The sugar syrup in this dressing makes it coat the salad much as would oil, and also tempers the heat of the chili paste.

Goulash

Chive Noodles

Sweet and Sour Cabbage

⌐

*H*earty cold–weather fare, this menu defies the notion that fat–free cooking can't produce stick–to–the–ribs food. Substituting turkey for beef in the goulash not only trims fat but also cuts down on the cooking time. Use good–quality Hungarian paprika for this Eastern European specialty. Most varieties of paprika sold in supermarkets tend to be mild, but more pungent paprikas often can be found in spice shops and ethnic groceries.

99% FAT–FREE FAST STRATEGY:

1. Prep the vegetables and turkey for the goulash. Preheat a saucepan.
2. Cook the goulash vegetables in the hot pan. Meanwhile, cook the cabbage.
3. Mix the additional ingredients into both the goulash and the cabbage. While both simmer, bring water to boil for the noodles.
4. Cook the noodles in the boiling water. Meanwhile, combine the cottage cheese and milk.
5. Finish the noodles.
6. Stir the cottage cheese and milk mixture into the goulash.
7. Divide the noodles among four dinner plates. Top each with 1 cup of goulash. Serve ½ cup cabbage per person on the side.

Goulash

5 ounces white onion (about 1 small onion)

4 ounces carrot (about 1 carrot)

1 clove garlic

8 ounces red bell pepper (about 1 pepper)

7 ounces turkey breast tenderloin

2 tablespoons water

½ cup canned diced tomatoes, drained

½ cup dry white wine

½ tablespoon paprika

½ teaspoon salt

½ teaspoon ground white pepper

½ teaspoon dried marjoram

1 teaspoon caraway seeds

½ cup nonfat cottage cheese

2 tablespoons skim milk

Peel and chunk the onion and carrot, peel the garlic, and trim and chunk the bell pepper. Combine in a food processor and pulse about 10 times to chop roughly. Cut the turkey into ¾-inch cubes. Meanwhile, preheat a medium nonstick saucepan over medium-high heat.

Transfer the vegetables to the hot pan. Add the water, cover, and cook for about 5 minutes, until the vegetables are limp and tender. Stir in the turkey, tomatoes, wine, and seasonings. Cover, reduce the heat to medium-low, and simmer for 15 minutes.

Combine the cottage cheese and milk in the food processor or blender and process or blend until smooth.

Remove the pan from the heat and whisk in the cottage cheese and milk mixture.

YIELD = 4 SERVINGS

Fat per serving = 1.00 g.

Calories per serving = 154.5

Sweet and Sour Cabbage

4 cups shredded red cabbage (precut)

¼ cup plus 2 tablespoons water

¼ cup plus 2 tablespoons red wine vinegar

2 tablespoons dark brown sugar

¼ teaspoon ground allspice

¼ teaspoon salt

Freshly ground black pepper to taste

In a large nonstick skillet, combine the cabbage and water. Cook over high heat for about 1 minute, until the cabbage begins to wilt. Stir in the remaining ingredients. Cover, reduce the heat to low, and simmer for about 15 minutes, until the cabbage is tender.

YIELD = 4 SERVINGS

Fat per serving = 0.21 g.

Calories per serving = 54.9

Chive Noodles

8 ounces yolkless broad noodles

2 tablespoons snipped fresh chives

Salt and freshly ground black pepper to taste

Bring a large saucepan of water to a boil over high heat. Stir in the noodles and cook for about 10 minutes, stirring occasionally, until tender but still firm to the touch.

Lightly drain the noodles, reserving ¼ cup of the cooking liquid. Return the noodles to the pan, along with the chives and the reserved liquid. Toss over high heat for a few seconds, until the liquid has been absorbed. Season with salt and pepper.

YIELD = 4 SERVINGS

Fat per serving = 0.50 g.

Calories per serving = 210.5

Don't be too compulsive about draining the noodles after boiling. You want some water still to be clinging to the noodles when you toss them with the chives, so that the chives will adhere.

Thai Chicken with Water Chestnuts and Broccoli
Endive and Watercress Salad

~

*O*ur spicy chicken derives its incendiary character from Thai roasted red chili paste, just one of the flavorful, low-fat Asian sauces that can now be found in the ethnic aisle of your local supermarket. The cool and crisp citrus salad would pair well with any highly seasoned dish. Sometimes we serve it with Spicy Turkey Curry (page 89) in lieu of the rice.

99% FAT-FREE FAST STRATEGY:
1. Make and dress the salad.
2. Prep the ingredients for the chicken dish.
3. While microwaving the broccoli, preheat a wok or skillet.
4. Make the chicken dish in the hot wok or skillet. Serve about 1 cup per person.

Endive and Watercress Salad

8 ounces Belgian endive (about 2 small heads)

6 ounces watercress (about 1 small bunch)

8 ounces navel orange (about 1 orange)

2 teaspoons Dijon mustard

¼ cup freshly squeezed lemon juice

2 tablespoons light corn syrup

No need to add pepper to this salad; it's peppery tasting enough from the watercress.

Trim and cut the endive into bite-sized pieces (about 2 cups). Remove the thick stems from the watercress and cut the leaves into bite-sized pieces (about 2 cups). Peel, trim, and cut the orange into bite-sized pieces (about 1 cup). Combine in a bowl and mix.

For the dressing, whisk the mustard and lemon juice together in a small bowl. Add the corn syrup and whisk until blended and frothy. Pour over the salad and toss.

YIELD = 4 SERVINGS

Fat per serving = 0.30 g.

Calories per serving = 66.5

We start with pretrimmed and washed broccoli florets to save prepping time, and then precook the broccoli in the microwave so that the sautéing will be quick and no oil need be added to the wok or skillet. If you don't have a microwave, bring a pot of water to a boil, blanch the broccoli florets in the boiling water until bright green but still crunchy, about 3 minutes, and refresh under cold running water.

7 ounces skinless, boneless chicken breast

1 tablespoon plus 2 teaspoons cornstarch

2 tablespoons reduced-sodium soy sauce

2 tablespoons white wine

4 ounces yellow onion (about 1 small onion)

2 pieces fresh ginger (each about the size of a quarter)

1 clove garlic

1 tablespoon Thai roasted red chili paste

1¼ cups plus 2 tablespoons chicken stock (see Pantry)

1½ cups broccoli florets (precut)

⅔ cup canned sliced water chestnuts, drained

Cut the chicken into ¼-inch cubes (about ⅔ cup). In a bowl, combine the chicken with a tablespoon of the cornstarch, 1 tablespoon of the soy sauce, and the white wine. Mix and set aside.

Peel and cut the onion into thin wedges (about 1 cup). Peel the ginger and the garlic.

In a small bowl, mix together the chili paste, the remaining 2 teaspoons of cornstarch, the remaining tablespoon of soy sauce, and 1 cup of the chicken stock.

Put the broccoli in a microwave-safe container, cover loosely with plastic wrap, and microwave at full power until lightly cooked but still firm, about 1 minute.

Preheat a nonstick wok or a large nonstick skillet over high heat. Combine ¼ cup of the remaining chicken stock, the ginger, and the garlic. Cook, stirring constantly, for 1 minute. Add the onion and continue to cook, stirring, for 1 minute more. Add the water chestnuts and cook and stir for about 30 seconds, until browned, then add the broccoli and cook and stir for 30 seconds more. Discard the ginger and garlic. Remove the remaining contents of the wok to a bowl.

Add the remaining 2 tablespoons of stock and the chicken to the wok or skillet. Cook for about 2 minutes, stirring constantly, until the chicken browns. Add the chili paste mixture and cook, stirring, for 1 minute to thicken. Add the reserved onion, broccoli, and water chestnut mixture. Toss to coat and cook and stir for 30 seconds more to heat through.

Serve about 1 cup per person.

YIELD = 4 SERVINGS

Fat per serving = 0.93 g.

Calories per serving = 117.5

Turkey Chili

Corn Muffins

—

*A*n eminently satisfying meal that's almost effortless, this is our favorite menu to accompany bowl games and inclement weather movie binges. We usually serve the chili in oversize mugs; for a more substantial sit-down presentation, serve it in pasta bowls over white rice. Because we add tomato paste and diced tomatoes, the chili thickens quickly and needs to simmer for only about 15 minutes.

99% FAT-FREE FAST STRATEGY:

1. Preheat the oven. Meanwhile, grease the muffin cups, mix the batter, and prep the vegetables and turkey for the chili.
2. Put the muffins into the oven and start cooking the chili.
3. Mix the additional ingredients into the chili and let simmer.
4. Remove the muffins and finish the chili.

Corn Muffins

Vegetable oil cooking spray

1 cup yellow cornmeal

1 cup all-purpose flour

1 tablespoon baking powder

1 teaspoon baking soda

3 tablespoons sugar

½ teaspoon salt

¼ teaspoon crushed red pepper

2 large egg whites

1½ cups buttermilk

¼ cup skim milk

1 cup frozen corn kernels

Preheat the oven to 425 degrees. Lightly coat the cups of a 12-cup muffin tin with vegetable oil cooking spray.

In a bowl, whisk together the cornmeal, flour, baking powder, baking soda, sugar, salt, and crushed red pepper. In a separate bowl, whisk the egg whites. Whisk in the buttermilk and skim milk. Whisk in the corn, then the mixed dry ingredients.

Divide the batter evenly among the cups of the prepared tin. Bake for about 20 minutes, until the muffins are firm to the touch and have browned on top.

YIELD = 12 MUFFINS

Fat per muffin = 0.62 g.

Calories per muffin = 117.2

Buttermilk lends these muffins the richness normally supplied by egg yolks and butter. We've found that a dozen muffins corresponds well to 8 servings of chili, as many guests will eat only a single muffin. If you're feeding the football team instead of watching it on television, the recipe can be doubled easily to provide a more-than-generous 3 muffins per person.

Turkey Chili

8 ounces red bell pepper (about 1 pepper)

8 ounces yellow bell pepper (about 1 pepper)

3 ounces celery (about 2 stalks)

9 ounces turkey breast tenderloin

One 15-ounce can black beans

1⅓ cups chopped white onion (precut)

½ tablespoon minced garlic (precut)

¼ cup water

1 tablespoon chili powder

2 teaspoons ground cumin

¼ teaspoon hot sauce (or to taste)

½ teaspoon ground black pepper

1 teaspoon salt

Two 15½-ounce cans diced tomatoes

1 cup frozen corn kernels

2 tablespoons tomato paste

2 tablespoons freshly squeezed lime juice

4 ounces fresh cilantro (about 1 bunch)

Trim and chop the bell peppers (about 2 cups) and the celery (about ⅔ cup). Cut the turkey into 1-×-½-inch pieces (about 1 cup). Rinse and drain the beans.

In a nonstick Dutch oven, combine the bell peppers, celery, onion, garlic, and water. Cook over medium heat for about 5 minutes, until the vegetables are limp.

Add the turkey and cook for about 1 minute, stirring constantly, until the meat is no longer pink. Add the seasonings, diced tomatoes, and beans. Raise the heat to high and bring to a boil. Cover, reduce the heat to medium-low, and simmer for 15 minutes.

Add the corn and tomato paste and cook for about 3 minutes more, uncovered, until thickened. Meanwhile, chop the cilantro (about ½ cup). Stir the lime juice and cilantro into the chili and serve.

YIELD = 8 SERVINGS

Fat per serving = 1.00 g.

Calories per serving = 114.4

Garlic Hoisin Shrimp

Hong Kong Slaw

Scallion Noodles

⁓

*G*arlic Hoisin Shrimp is the ultimate rich, garlicky, full-flavored Chinese dish. Serve it alongside the flavorful noodles. If desired, garnish the shrimp and the noodles with a light sprinkling of chopped basil. The slaw can be served at the same time, on a separate plate, or as a first course. In both the slaw and the noodles, we use just a tad of highly flavorful but also high-in-fat sesame oil.

Sometimes we pair Hong Kong Slaw with Mahimahi Burgers (page 171) for variety. Conversely, you could serve the Coleslaw (page 172) that usually accompanies the burgers with this menu; this is a good option if you have trouble finding the napa cabbage used for Hong Kong Slaw.

99% FAT-FREE FAST STRATEGY:

1. Prep the leek, bell pepper, ginger, and garlic.
2. Marinate the shrimp.
3. Make the slaw and plate it atop the cabbage leaves.
4. Make the garlic sauce for the shrimp. Chop the scallions for the noodles.
5. Put water up to boil for the noodles. Preheat a wok or skillet.
6. Add the stock to the hot pan and cook the vegetables for the shrimp dish. Remove the vegetables to a bowl.
7. Reheat the pan. Add the shrimp, then the sauce, and finish cooking. Remove from the heat and stir in the vegetables.
8. Cook the noodles in the boiling water. Remove to a bowl and toss with sesame oil and scallions.

Garlic Hoisin Shrimp

Hoisin sauce is sold both in glass jars and in plastic squeeze bottles; the thicker variety that comes in a jar is preferable for this recipe.

4 ounces leek (about 1 thin leek)

7 ounces red bell pepper (about 1 pepper)

4 pieces fresh ginger (each about the size of a quarter)

4 cloves garlic

6 ounces peeled, deveined medium shrimp

2 tablespoons dry sherry

1 tablespoon plus 1 teaspoon cornstarch

2½ tablespoons reduced-sodium soy sauce

⅔ cup plus ¼ cup shrimp or vegetable stock (see Pantry)

2 tablespoons Chinese hoisin sauce

2 tablespoons chopped fresh basil leaves

½ teaspoon chopped garlic (precut)

8 ounces fresh sugar snap peas (about 2 cups)

½ cup sliced canned bamboo shoots, drained

Trim the leek to the white and some light green parts. Cut it in half lengthwise, clean, and slice thin (about ½ cup). Trim and cut the bell pepper into 3-× ¼-inch strips. Peel the ginger. Peel and smash the garlic cloves; set them aside.

In a small bowl, combine the shrimp, sherry, 1 teaspoon of the cornstarch, and 1½ tablespoons of the soy sauce. Mix well and set aside to marinate.

Make the sauce in a second bowl: Combine ⅔ cup of the stock, the hoisin sauce, the remaining tablespoon of cornstarch, the remaining tablespoon of soy sauce, the basil, and chopped garlic. Mix and set aside.

Heat a wok or a large nonstick skillet over high heat.

Add the remaining ¼ cup of stock. When the stock is steamy, add the ginger and the smashed garlic cloves. Continue to cook until about half the stock has evaporated, then add the sugar snap peas, leek, and bell pepper. Cook for about 2 minutes, stirring constantly, until the vegetables are lightly browned and all of the stock has been absorbed. Add the bamboo shoots and cook just to warm, stirring, about 10 seconds. Discard the ginger and garlic cloves and remove the remaining contents to a bowl.

Reheat the wok or skillet. Add the shrimp and their marinade. Cook and stir for about 1 minute, until the shrimp are opaque. Add the sauce and stir to dissolve any marinade that may have congealed. Cook for about 30 seconds more, stirring, until the liquid thickens, bubbles, and turns clear. Remove from the heat and stir in the vegetables.

Serve about 1 cup per person.

YIELD = 4 SERVINGS

Fat per serving = 0.51 g.

Calories per serving = 136.0

Hong Kong Slaw

10 ounces napa cabbage

2 scallions

1 tablespoon rice wine vinegar

1½ tablespoons reduced-sodium soy sauce

½ tablespoon sugar

¼ teaspoon sesame oil

1 teaspoon grated ginger (precut)

Remove and reserve 4 whole cabbage leaves; core and thinly slice the remainder (about 2 cups). Trim the scallions, leaving only about 3 inches of the dark green ends, and chop (about 2 tablespoons). Combine the cabbage and scallions in a bowl and mix.

In a small bowl, combine the remaining ingredients and mix. Pour the dressing over the cabbage and toss to coat. Serve ½ cup per person over a single cabbage leaf on each of 4 salad plates.

YIELD = 4 SERVINGS

Fat per serving = 0.42 g.

Calories per serving = 18.0

Scallion Noodles

2 scallions

6 ounces fresh chow mein noodles

¼ teaspoon sesame oil

Chop the scallions (about 2 tablespoons).

Fill a large saucepan about two thirds full with water and bring it to a boil over high heat. Add the noodles, stir to separate them, and cook for 1 minute. With a slotted spoon, transfer the noodles to a bowl. Add the sesame oil and scallions and toss well.

YIELD = 4 SERVINGS

Fat per serving = 0.82 g.

Calories per serving = 128.8

Buy fresh chow mein noodles—sold in the produce section alongside won ton and egg roll wrappers—not the canned, fried variety. Leave a little water clinging to the noodles when you remove them from the pot.

Thanksgiving Turkey with Vegetables à la W. R.
Potato-Fennel Gratin

~

*T*his quick fat–free feast was inspired by a wonderful Thanksgiving menu of William Rice's. Bill developed his simple, elegant presentation of poached turkey and vegetables with gravy for folks whose lifestyles don't lend them–selves to spending days preparing the gargantuan, high–fat and high–calorie spreads typically associated with holiday overindulgence. We've attempted to adapt the concept to fit our own time and fat parameters—using a leaner cut of turkey, trimming the skin, and consolidating steps—without sacrific–ing flavor.

We serve the turkey and vegetable main course along with a rich gratin of potato and fennel, thickened with buttermilk instead of butter and cream and cooked in a hot oven in about half the normal time. We love to finish the feast with a flourish—Carrot Soufflé with Carrot Sauce (page 174), our modern, elegant answer to pumpkin pie.

99% FAT–FREE FAST STRATEGY:
1. Preheat the oven. Meanwhile, prep and microwave the fennel. Layer the gratin, put it into the oven to bake, and proceed with the menu.
2. While bringing the stock to boil in a skillet, prep the vegetables.
3. Simmer the turkey, onions, and carrots in the hot stock.
4. Add the remaining vegetables to the skillet and continue to cook.
5. Remove the skillet from the heat and the gratin from the oven. Make the gravy.
6. Slice the turkey. Serve about five slices on each of four dinner plates, surround with vegetables, and drizzle with gravy. Slice and serve the gratin on the side.

Potato-Fennel Gratin

1 pound fennel (about 1 bulb)

½ tablespoon chopped garlic (precut)

1 pound refrigerated sliced home fries (about 2 packed cups)

Salt and freshly ground black pepper to taste

⅔ cup buttermilk

⅓ cup bread crumbs (see Pantry)

Preheat the oven to 450 degrees.

Trim the fennel, cut it in half lengthwise, core, and slice thin (about 3 cups). Put it into a shallow microwave-safe bowl and cover loosely with plastic wrap. Microwave at full power for about 3 minutes, until heated through and softened.

Transfer half the fennel to a 9-inch round nonstick cake pan or gratin dish and pat it with a spatula into a smooth layer. Spread ¾ teaspoon of the garlic on top, add the potatoes in a layer, and spread the remaining ¾ teaspoon of garlic over the potatoes. Add a final layer of the remaining fennel. Season with salt and pepper, pour the buttermilk over the gratin, and top with the bread crumbs.

Bake for about 20 minutes, until the gratin has browned on top and is fork tender inside.

YIELD = 4 SERVINGS

Fat per serving = 0.60 g.

Calories per serving = 132.2

For this remarkably quick and easy holiday gratin, look for sliced home fries (peeled and precut potatoes) in your supermarket's refrigerator case.

Thanksgiving Turkey with Vegetables à la W. R.

*O*ur festive spread of turkey and vegetables is topped with a light stock and tarragon gravy thickened with just a bit of cornstarch. Use all chicken stock, all vegetable stock, or any combination thereof.

3⅓ cups chicken and/or vegetable stock (see Pantry)

4 ounces pearl onions (about 16 onions)

4 ounces white button mushrooms (about 8 mushrooms)

8 ounces zucchini (about 1 large zucchini)

9 ounces turkey breast tenderloin

3 ounces baby-cut carrots (precut; about 20 carrots)

½ tablespoon chopped fresh tarragon

1 tablespoon cornstarch

Salt and freshly ground black pepper to taste

In a medium nonstick skillet, bring the stock to a boil over high heat.

Meanwhile, peel the onions. Trim, clean, and quarter the mushrooms. Trim the zucchini, cut it into thirds crosswise, then quarter each third lengthwise.

Put the turkey in the center of the skillet and add the onions and carrots around the sides. Cover, reduce the heat to medium-low, and simmer for 7 minutes.

Add the mushrooms and zucchini to the skillet. Re-cover and cook for about 8 minutes until the turkey is firm and the vegetables fork tender. Remove from the heat.

To make the gravy, transfer 1 cup of the stock from the skillet to a small saucepan. Add the tarragon and bring to a boil over high heat. Meanwhile, remove another ¼ cup of stock to a small bowl and mix in the cornstarch. Remove the boiling stock from the heat and stir in the cornstarch mixture. Return the pan to the heat and cook, stirring constantly, for about 2 minutes, until the gravy begins to thicken and boil. Season with salt and pepper. Slice the turkey thin (about 20 slices).

YIELD = 4 SERVINGS

Fat per serving = 0.99 g.

Calories per serving = 114.6

Menus
for
Lunches,
Brunches,
and Casual Dinners

Chunky Tomato Potato-Fennel Soup
Smoked Sturgeon Wraps

⌒

*W*e pair our novel and abundantly stuffed wraps, inspired by a traditional Scandinavian potato and sturgeon salad, with an equally rich and filling soup. We prefer to make the wraps while the soup simmers and serve them together, but you could easily serve the meal in courses.

Those with less hearty appetites might want to serve the wraps with only a salad on the side; either the Watercress and Carrot Salad (page 37) or the Endive and Watercress Salad (page 119) would go nicely. On its own, the soup makes a warming and substantial winter lunch.

99% FAT-FREE FAST STRATEGY:
1. Prep and microwave the fennel for the soup.
2. For the wraps, prep the cucumber and microwave the potatoes.
3. Combine the soup ingredients and simmer.
4. Blend the ricotta cheese mixture for the wraps in a food processor.
5. Mix the filling and assemble the wraps.

Chunky Tomato Potato-Fennel Soup

6 ounces fennel

One 14½-ounce can diced tomatoes with garlic, basil, and oregano

1½ cups chicken stock (see Pantry)

4 ounces frozen hash brown potatoes (about 1 cup)

½ cup evaporated skim milk

1 tablespoon sliced fresh basil leaves

Trim the fennel to the white part only, reserving the feathery leaves for garnish, and dice (about 1¼ cups). Drain the tomatoes.

Combine the fennel and ½ cup of the chicken stock in a microwave-safe bowl. Cover tightly with plastic wrap and heat for 2 minutes at full power, until the mixture is steaming and the fennel is beginning to soften. Transfer it to a large nonstick saucepan and add the potatoes, tomatoes, and the remaining cup of chicken stock. Bring to a boil over high heat, reduce the heat to medium, and simmer for 5 minutes.

Remove the pan from the heat and stir in the evaporated milk and the basil. Ladle 1 cup into each of 4 soup bowls and garnish with the reserved fennel leaves.

YIELD = 4 SERVINGS

Fat per serving = 0.16 g.

Calories per serving = 94.0

The growing selection of peeled, precut, and ready-to-cook potatoes, both refrigerated and frozen, is a boon to any time-constrained cook. Don't be deterred by such terms as "hash browns" or "home fries" on the package, which refer only to the manner in which the potatoes are cut. In this recipe, we use a frozen product diced in typical hash-brown fashion; for the wraps, we use a refrigerated product, also labeled as hash browns, whose shredded form is better suited to the recipe.

This is a very thick and chunky soup. For a smoother soup, puree before serving. For a thinner and smoother soup, add more chicken stock while pureeing, then reheat until steaming.

Smoked Sturgeon Wraps

You want to use smoked sturgeon sliced as thin as possible in these generously stuffed wraps. Sturgeon is now available presliced and vacuum-packed in better markets; look in the refrigerated fish section.

Serve sliced tomato and onion on the side, if you wish.

10 ounces cucumber (about 1 cucumber)

6 tablespoons prepared horseradish

¼ cup water

1 pound refrigerated shredded hash brown potatoes (about 2 cups)

1 tablespoon finely snipped fresh chives

1 cup skim milk ricotta cheese

2 tablespoons freshly squeezed lemon juice

Four 9-inch nonfat flour tortillas

Salt and freshly ground black pepper to taste

4 ounces sliced smoked sturgeon (about 6 large slices)

Peel and chop the cucumber (about 1 cup). Drain the horseradish.

Combine the water and potatoes in a microwave-safe bowl and cover loosely with plastic wrap. Microwave for about 2 minutes at full power, until the potatoes are steaming. Remove and fluff with a fork.

Transfer the potatoes to a bowl and add the cucumber and chives.

In a food processor, combine the ricotta cheese, lemon juice, and horseradish. Process for about 20 seconds, until well blended and smooth. (You should have about 1¼ cups of the mixture.) Spread 1 tablespoon on each of the tortillas and add the remainder to the bowl with the potatoes and cucumber. Stir to combine. Season with salt and pepper.

Place 1½ slices of the smoked sturgeon in the center of each tortilla. Top each with about ¾ cup of the potato mixture. Fold 2 opposite sides of each tortilla over the filling and then roll up, starting with a short end.

YIELD = 4 SERVINGS

Fat per serving = 0.79 g.

Calories per serving = 294.0

Creamy Ginger-Tomato Soup

Smoked Scallop Hash

~

*O*ld-fashioned comfort food with some elegant, updated touches, we think of this menu as the perfect light yet satisfying Sunday–night supper. For a change of pace, try the hash made with other types of smoked fish, such as trout or whitefish. We like to serve it up in the traditional manner, with chili sauce on the side.

99% FAT–FREE FAST STRATEGY:

1. Prep the potatoes, mushrooms, and scallops for the hash.
2. Microwave the potatoes.
3. While preheating a skillet for the hash, start the soup.
4. While the soup heats, cook the hash in the hot skillet.
5. Finish and garnish the soup.

Smoked Scallop Hash

Look for smoked scallops, which come vacuum-packed, in the seafood section of better supermarkets.

1 pound red potatoes (2 to 3 potatoes)

4 ounces white button mushrooms

6 ounces smoked scallops

½ cup water

1 cup chopped white onion (precut)

2 teaspoons fresh thyme leaves, or ½ teaspoon dried thyme

⅔ cup evaporated skim milk

¼ teaspoon salt

¼ teaspoon ground white pepper

Peel and cube the potatoes (about 2 cups). Trim, clean, and cube the mushrooms (about 1 cup). Shred the scallops (about ⅔ cup).

Combine the potatoes and water in a microwave-safe bowl. Cover with plastic wrap and microwave at full power for 2½ to 3 minutes, until the potatoes are fork tender.

Preheat a medium nonstick skillet over medium heat.

Drain the potatoes of any residual water. Combine the potatoes, onion, mushrooms, scallops, thyme, and evaporated milk in the hot skillet. Cook for 3 to 4 minutes, stirring constantly, until all the milk has been absorbed.

Stir in the salt and pepper.

YIELD = 4 SERVINGS

Fat per serving = 0.61 g.

Calories per serving = 156.6

Creamy Ginger-Tomato Soup

4 cups boxed strained tomatoes (such as Pomi)

½ cup evaporated skim milk

¼ cup plus 2 tablespoons grated ginger (precut)

Salt and freshly ground black pepper to taste

Snipped fresh chives for garnish

In a medium saucepan, combine the tomatoes and evaporated milk. Wrap the ginger in paper toweling and squeeze the juice into the pan. Cook over medium heat for 4 to 5 minutes, stirring occasionally, until steaming.

Season with salt and pepper. Ladle 1 cup into each of 4 soup bowls and garnish with the chives.

YIELD = 4 SERVINGS

Fat per serving = 0.14 g.

Calories per serving = 110.1

It takes all of 5 minutes to make this terrific-tasting soup from scratch! By squeezing the juice from grated ginger into the pot, you capture the robust flavor with no floating bits of ginger to distract from the silky smoothness of the soup. Use the best-quality strained tomatoes you can find; we're particularly fond of the pure variety from Italy that can now be found in a box in many supermarkets.

White Bean and Sausage Soup
Tuna Niçoise Wraps

~

*T*his highly versatile menu includes a hearty bowl of soup and a substantial sandwich. Either can be eaten alone for a lighter repast or paired with something else—try the wraps with Yellow Chowder (page 147), Creamy Tomato–Ginger Soup (page 139), Watercress and Carrot Salad (page 37), or Endive and Watercress Salad (page 119), or the soup with Tomato Bread (page 97) or a homemade baguette fresh from the oven (see Pantry).

99% FAT-FREE FAST STRATEGY:

1. Prep the carrot, turkey sausage, and escarole and start to cook the soup.
2. Mix the additional ingredients into the soup and let it simmer. Meanwhile, prep the ingredients for the wraps and puree the spread.
3. Puree some of the contents of the soup pot as a thickener and return to the pan, along with the final additions.
4. While the soup finishes cooking, assemble the wraps.

White Bean and Sausage Soup

One 15-ounce can navy beans

4 ounces carrot (about 1 carrot)

2 ounces smoked turkey sausage

1 pound escarole (about 1 head)

1 cup chopped white onion (precut)

1 teaspoon minced garlic (precut)

2 tablespoons water

½ teaspoon dried thyme

1 bay leaf

2 cups chicken stock (see Pantry)

Salt and freshly ground black pepper to
taste

Rinse and drain the beans.

Chop the carrot (about ⅓ cup) and the turkey sausage (about ¼ cup). Trim and chop the escarole (about 5 cups).

In a large saucepan, combine the carrot, onion, garlic, and water. Cook over medium–high heat for about 5 minutes, until dry and limp. Stir in the beans, thyme, and bay leaf. Pour in the chicken stock and bring to a boil. Cover, reduce the heat to low, and simmer for about 15 minutes, until the vegetables can be mashed easily.

Remove the bay leaf.

Transfer 2 cups of vegetables and stock to a food processor or blender and puree until smooth. Return the puree to the pan. Stir in the sausage and escarole. Cook for about 5 minutes more, until the escarole is wilted and tender. Season with salt and pepper.

Ladle 1¼ cups into each of 4 soup bowls.

YIELD = 4 SERVINGS

Fat per serving = 0.78 g.

Calories per serving = 158.5

Tuna Niçoise Wraps

To pare fat grams, we use capers instead of olives and anchovy paste instead of whole fillets, which we combine with garlic and roasted red peppers in a fresh and aromatic relish. If you're lucky enough to find *haricots verts*, the delicate French beans, in your market, parboil a few for a terrific addition to the wraps.

One 6-ounce can solid white albacore tuna in water

6 ounces sweet roasted peppers (preroasted)

6 ounces tomato (about 1 tomato)

4 ounces white onion

2 teaspoons drained capers

2 teaspoons minced roasted garlic (precut)

¾ teaspoon anchovy paste

Two 9-inch rounds Armenian flatbread

4 leaves romaine lettuce

Drain the tuna. Drain the roasted peppers and cut them into large pieces. Core the tomato and cut it crosswise into 4 slices. Cut the onion into 2 slices, then cut each slice in half.

In a food processor or blender, combine the capers, roasted peppers, roasted garlic, and anchovy paste and puree to a chunky consistency (about ½ cup).

Spread 2 tablespoons of the puree on each round of flatbread and cover with 2 lettuce leaves. Top 1 leaf on each round with 2 slices of tomato, half the tuna, 2 pieces of onion, and 2 tablespoons of the remaining puree. Fold each round over the filling, cut it in half, and secure closed with toothpicks.

YIELD = 4 SERVINGS

Fat per serving = 1.00 g.

Calories per serving = 145.5

Scallop and Smoked Turkey Jambalaya
Sautéed Chard

~

*W*e had to work hard to top the Shrimp Jambalaya in our original *99% Fat-Free Cookbook,* but we think we've succeeded. This dish is an ultimate fat-free fast recipe—minimal work, minimal time, minimal fat. We replace the rice and shrimp of our original recipe with fast-cooking couscous and bay scallops, trimming a whole fifteen minutes off the cooking time!

The jambalaya has a traditional smoky taste, lent by the smoked turkey sausage. It's paired with a simple presentation of red chard tossed in balsamic vinegar, which we predict will become a favorite in your own minimal preparation, minimal fat kitchen. The combination of chard and vinegar is assertive enough to stand up to as robust a dish as jambalaya, yet it can also serve to enliven plain broiled, grilled, or steamed fish or poultry.

99% FAT-FREE FAST STRATEGY:

1. Prep the celery, turkey, and scallops for the jambalaya. Meanwhile, preheat a skillet.
2. Begin to cook the jambalaya in the hot skillet, stirring frequently.
3. Stir in the next few ingredients and bring to a boil.
4. Mix in the remaining ingredients, cover, and set aside off the heat.
5. While the jambalaya steeps, preheat a sauté pan and cook the chard in the hot pan.
6. Fluff and serve the jambalaya, with the chard on the side.

In this recipe, tiny bay scallops cook in no time off the stovetop in the heat from the stock; if you substitute sea scallops, quarter them first.

Scallop and Smoked Turkey Jambalaya

6 ounces green bell pepper (about 1 pepper)

2 ounces celery (about 1 large stalk)

2 ounces smoked turkey sausage

One 14½-ounce can diced tomatoes

1 tablespoon minced garlic (precut)

1 cup chopped white onion (precut)

1 teaspoon dried thyme

1½ cups chicken stock (see Pantry)

½ teaspoon Worcestershire sauce

½ teaspoon hot sauce

10 ounces bay scallops

1 cup quick-cooking couscous

Trim and chop the green pepper (about ¾ cup) and celery (about ⅓ cup). Chop the smoked turkey sausage (about ¼ cup). Drain the tomatoes.

Preheat a large nonstick skillet over medium heat. Combine the bell pepper, celery, garlic, and onion in the hot skillet. Cook for about 5 minutes, stirring frequently, until the onion begins to turn golden. Stir in the tomatoes, sausage, and thyme. Add the chicken stock, Worcestershire sauce, and hot sauce. Raise the heat to high and bring to a boil. Stir in the scallops, then the couscous.

Cover, remove from the heat, and set aside for 5 minutes. Stir and fluff with a fork. Serve about 1½ cups per person.

YIELD = 4 SERVINGS

Fat per serving = 0.99 g.

Calories per serving = 277.1

Sautéed Chard

12 ounces red chard (about 1 bunch)   2 tablespoons balsamic vinegar

Trim and cut the chard into large pieces (about 6 cups).

Preheat a heavy, nonstick sauté pan over high heat. Pour the vinegar into the hot pan and place the chard on top. Toss to coat, cover, and cook for about 1 minute, just until the chard is wilted. Toss again.

YIELD = 4 SERVINGS

Fat per serving = 0.15 g.

Calories per serving = 16.2

We think red chard, also called "rhubarb chard," is one of the most overlooked of vegetables. It is much more flavorful than Swiss chard, and its dark green leaves and red ribs add colorful appeal to the plate.

Yellow Chowder

Grilled Vegetable Hoagie with Garlic Spread

⁓

*T*his is a perfect menu for a casual dinner or lunch. It features a substantial sandwich and a creamy chowder made without any cream—pureed corn lending much the same color and texture in this recipe. Omitting the cream allows us to add a dollop of shrimp to each serving for visual contrast and heightened flavor. We hollow out the French bread for our hoagies to make them less unwieldy; you get a mouthful of veggies instead of dough with every bite.

99% FAT-FREE FAST STRATEGY:

1. Start the chowder; while the squash and corn simmer, make the garlic spread and preheat the grill or broiler.
2. Prep the eggplant, zucchini, and mushrooms for grilling or broiling.
3. Puree the chowder; return it to the pan and keep warm over low heat.
4. Grill or broil the vegetables; meanwhile, prep the French bread, roasted peppers, and tomatoes.
5. Assemble the sandwiches and garnish the chowder.

Yellow Chowder

6 ounces yellow summer squash (also called "crookneck squash"; about 1 squash)

1 ounce cooked, peeled medium shrimp

2½ cups frozen corn kernels

3 cups chicken stock (see Pantry)

½ teaspoon dried thyme

¼ teaspoon ground black pepper

½ teaspoon salt

2 teaspoons snipped fresh chives for garnish

Peel, trim, and chop the squash (about 1½ cups) and chop the shrimp (about ½ cup).

In a large saucepan, combine the squash, corn, and chicken stock. Cover and bring to a boil over high heat. Reduce the heat to medium−low and simmer for about 15 minutes, until the vegetables can be mashed easily with a fork.

Transfer the contents of the pan to a food processor or blender and puree until smooth. Add the seasonings and pulse to mix. Return the puree to the saucepan and reheat.

Ladle 1 cup of chowder into each of 4 soup bowls. Put 2 tablespoons chopped shrimp in the center of each and scatter ½ teaspoon of chives on top.

YIELD = 4 SERVINGS

Fat per serving = 0.70 g.

Calories per serving = 106.7

A bit of chopped shrimp as garnish lends an elegant finishing touch to this dish, but the chowder is equally tasty without it.

Garlic Spread

We put this tasty and versatile spread to a lot of uses beyond our Grilled Vegetable Hoagies. It's also delicious on a smoked turkey and tomato sandwich. As a dressing, it can be drizzled with equal success over a salad of purple onions and tomatoes or a plate of steamed vegetables. We use it to dress our Fennel and Artichoke Heart Salad (page 165) and sometimes on our Couscous Salad (page 78) in lieu of blue cheese dressing.

¼ cup nonfat cottage cheese

1 tablespoon skim milk

½ teaspoon minced garlic (precut)

1 teaspoon freshly squeezed lemon juice

¼ teaspoon paprika

⅛ teaspoon cayenne pepper

In a food processor or blender, combine the cottage cheese and skim milk and puree until smooth. Add the remaining ingredients and process or blend just to combine.

YIELD = ABOUT ¼ CUP

Fat per tablespoon = 0.10 g.

Calories per tablespoon = 13.2

Grilled Vegetable Hoagie

8 ounces purple eggplant

12 ounces zucchini (about 2 zucchini)

6 ounces portobello mushrooms (about four 4-inch diameter mushrooms)

One 12-ounce jar sweet roasted peppers

One 14-inch loaf French bread

12 ounces tomatoes (about 2 tomatoes)

¼ cup Garlic Spread (page 148)

1 tablespoon chopped fresh basil leaves

Preheat the grill or broiler. (If grilling on other than a nonstick surface, coat the grill lightly with vegetable oil cooking spray. If broiling, line the pan, to be positioned 2 inches from the heat source, with aluminum foil.)

Trim and cut the eggplant into eight ½-inch-thick rounds. Trim and cut the zucchini into sixteen ¼-inch-thick rounds. Trim, clean, and halve the mushrooms. Rinse and drain the roasted peppers.

Grill or broil the eggplant, zucchini, and mushrooms in a single layer for 3 to 4 minutes on each side, until lightly browned.

Meanwhile, quarter the loaf of bread and cut each quarter open. Scoop out as much dough as can easily be removed to form deep wells in both the bottom and top halves. Cut each roasted pepper open lengthwise, then cut it in half crosswise. Trim and cut each tomato into 4 slices.

Coat each slice of bread with ½ tablespoon of the garlic spread. Lay 2 pieces of roasted pepper on each of the 4 bottom slices. Layer each sandwich with 2 pieces of mushroom, 2 eggplant rounds, and 4 zucchini rounds. Add 2 slices of tomato to each and sprinkle with ¾ teaspoon of basil. Cover with the 4 top slices of bread.

YIELD = 4 SERVINGS

Fat per serving = 0.84 g. (including spread)

Calories per serving = 247.1 (including spread)

If you haven't yet discovered preroasted peppers in the jar, which can be found in the Italian food section of your supermarket, be sure to try them out in this recipe. Both sweet and hot peppers are now available in preroasted form. They're virtually indistinguishable from those you've made from scratch, eliminating a good 15 to 20 minutes of cumbersome roasting, cooling, and peeling.

Smoked Turkey Roll-Ups
Refried Black Beans
Citrus Salsa

~

*F*or this light and healthy Mexican dinner, we replace the usual kidney or pinto beans with black beans and dispense with the fat in which they typically are fried. The menu features a thoroughly modern and refreshing citrus salsa, but includes the traditional Mexican soft taco instead of the crisp, fried version popularized by fast food vendors. There's not a single shred of iceberg lettuce in sight; we prefer to garnish the roll-ups with the artichoke hearts that are heated with the smoked turkey filling.

99% FAT-FREE FAST STRATEGY:

1. Make the citrus salsa and refrigerate it until ready to serve.
2. Cook the beans and keep them warm over very low heat.
3. Prep the turkey for the roll-ups.
4. Warm the tortillas in a microwave oven and preheat a skillet.
5. Cook the turkey and other filling ingredients in the hot skillet.
6. Assemble the roll-ups.
7. Stir the store-bought salsa into the refried beans.
8. Place two roll-ups in the center of each of four dinner plates and surround with about 1/4 cup refried beans and 1/2 cup citrus salsa.

Citrus Salsa

One 26-ounce jar unsweetened pink
   grapefruit segments

1 ounce jicama

2 ounces fresh cilantro

¼ teaspoon crushed red pepper

2 teaspoons pure clover honey

2 tablespoons freshly squeezed lime juice

Coarsely chop the grapefruit segments (about 2 generous cups). Peel and dice the ji-cama (about ½ cup). Chop the cilantro (about ¼ cup).

    In a bowl, combine the grapefruit, jicama, cilantro, crushed red pepper, honey, and lime juice. Stir to mix. Cover and refrigerate until ready to serve.

YIELD = 4 SERVINGS

Fat per serving = 0.17 g.

Calories per serving = 52.9

This salsa is also wonderful atop almost any grilled or baked fish. Look for grapefruit segments packed in natural juice, not syrup; in our supermarket, they can be found in the produce section.

Refried Black Beans

One 15½-ounce can black beans
¼ cup water

2 tablespoons store-bought salsa

Rinse and drain the beans.

In a small nonstick skillet, combine the beans and water. Cook over medium-high heat for about 5 minutes, periodically stirring and mashing the beans, until thoroughly mashed. Keep warm over *very* low heat until ready to serve.

Raise the heat to low and stir in the salsa.

YIELD = 4 SERVINGS

Fat per serving = 0.38 g.
Calories per serving = 87.3

You can substitute chicken or vegetable stock for the water for a slightly richer taste. Use a red salsa rather than the Citrus Salsa in the refried beans. It's really not necessary to start from scratch for the small amount called for here; select a chunky, high-quality salsa.

Smoked Turkey Roll-Ups

6 ounces skinless smoked turkey breast

Eight 7-inch corn tortillas

½ tablespoon chopped jalapeño pepper
    (precut)

2 tablespoons chopped fresh cilantro

One 9-ounce package frozen artichoke
    hearts, thawed

2 tablespoons water

Shred the turkey (about 1 cup).

Wrap the tortillas in damp paper toweling and microwave at full power for about 45 seconds. Keep them wrapped until ready to use. Meanwhile, preheat a medium nonstick skillet over high heat.

Combine the turkey, jalapeño pepper, cilantro, artichoke hearts, and water in the hot skillet. Cook for about 2 minutes, stirring constantly, until the water has been absorbed and the mixture heated thoroughly.

Unwrap the tortillas. Mound ¼ cup of the turkey mixture on each tortilla and roll each one into a cylinder.

YIELD = 4 SERVINGS

Fat per serving = 0.73 g.

Calories per serving = 163.9

We warm the tortillas in a microwave because it's so convenient, but you can also use a conventional oven at its lowest setting. We usually serve the beans next to the roll-ups; for variety, spread the beans on the tortillas before they are filled.

Thai Tilapia Curry
Curried Rice

~

*T*his is one of our favorite menus because it is so easy and so versatile. You can replace the tilapia with turkey breast tenderloin, chicken breast, shrimp, or scallops, and alter the character of the dishes at whim by using different types of curry powder. We like to garnish the curry with mango chutney and follow with Piña Colada Sherbet (page 187) for dessert.

99% FAT–FREE FAST STRATEGY:

1. Put the rice up to cook.
2. Meanwhile, prep the vegetables and the fish for the tilapia curry and make the curry sauce.
3. Preheat a wok or skillet for the curried rice.
4. Combine the flavorings for the curried rice. Add the flavorings and then the cooked rice to the hot wok or skillet and heat. Cover and set aside until ready to serve.
5. Preheat a wok or skillet for the tilapia curry.
6. Make the curry.
7. On each of four dinner plates, serve 1 cup of the curry and ¾ cup of curried rice. Garnish with cilantro.

Curried Rice

For a slightly sweeter rendition, add ½ cup golden raisins along with the cooked rice to the steaming coconut-milk mixture in the wok.

2 cups water

1 cup long-grain white rice

3 tablespoons light coconut milk

1 tablespoon reduced-sodium soy sauce

1 tablespoon dry sherry

1 tablespoon vegetable stock (see Pantry) or water

1 tablespoon grated ginger (precut)

2 teaspoons minced roasted garlic (precut)

½ tablespoon curry powder (see Pantry)

In a medium saucepan, bring the 2 cups water to a boil. Stir in the rice, reduce the heat to low, cover, and simmer for 15 minutes.

Combine the remaining ingredients in a bowl and mix well.

Preheat a nonstick wok or a large nonstick skillet over high heat. When the rice is done, add the coconut milk mixture to the wok or skillet and heat until steaming, about 5 seconds. Add the rice to the pan, stir to coat, and cook for about 2 minutes, until crusty. Remove from the heat and cover until ready to serve.

YIELD = 4 SERVINGS

Fat per serving = 0.70 g.

Calories per serving = 73.6

Thai Tilapia Curry

Not only are sugar snap peas tasty, but they're also—well—a snap to use. They are ready to eat as sold in the market, with no prepping needed. The biggest hazard of cooking with sugar snap peas is that you could easily eat them all right out of the bag before they find their way into the curry.

5 ounces red bell pepper (about 1 small pepper)

4 ounces scallions (about 4 large scallions)

12 ounces tilapia

¼ ounce fresh ginger

2 cloves garlic

2 ounces fresh cilantro

1 cup shrimp or vegetable stock (see Pantry)

1 tablespoon light coconut milk

1 teaspoon reduced–sodium soy sauce

1¾ teaspoons curry powder (see Pantry)

2 teaspoons cornstarch

4 ounces fresh sugar snap peas (about 1 cup)

Trim and cut the bell pepper into thin strips (about 1⅓ cups). Trim the scallions, leaving only about 3 inches of the dark green ends, and cut on a severe diagonal into 1–inch pieces (about ½ cup). Cut the tilapia into 1–inch cubes. Peel and slice the ginger (about 4 slices) and peel and halve the garlic. Chop the cilantro (about ¼ cup).

For the sauce, in a bowl, combine ½ cup of the stock, the coconut milk, soy sauce, curry powder, and cornstarch and mix to dissolve completely.

Preheat a nonstick wok or a large nonstick skillet over high heat. Put ¼ cup of the stock into the hot pan, along with the ginger and garlic. Add the sugar snap peas and bell pepper and cook, stirring, for 1 minute. Add the scallions and cook for about 30 seconds more, stirring, until the scallions turn bright green and the stock evaporates. Discard the ginger and garlic. Remove the vegetables to a bowl.

Put the remaining ¼ cup of stock into the wok or skillet and heat for 10 seconds over high heat. Add the tilapia. Cook, stirring, for about 1 minute, until the fish turns opaque. Add the reserved sauce and continue to cook and stir until it thickens and turns bubbly. Return the vegetables to the pan and toss to coat with the sauce.

Serve the curry with the curried rice and garnish it with the chopped cilantro.

YIELD = 4 SERVINGS

Fat per serving = 0.99 g.

Calories per serving = 117.4

White Gazpacho
Turkey Caesar Salad

~

*T*ogether, these dishes make a perfect light dinner or an excellent menu for lunch or brunch. They can also be mixed and matched with heavier main course fare, using the gazpacho as a first course or the salad as a side dish. The gazpacho is best the day it's made; the Caesar dressing for the salad holds up nicely overnight in the refrigerator.

99% Fat–Free Fast Strategy:
1. Preheat the broiler. Meanwhile, make the gazpacho; refrigerate until ready to serve.
2. While broiling the turkey, heat the tortillas and prep the roasted peppers and garlic for the salad. Remove the turkey and turn the oven down.
3. Make the salad dressing.
4. Bake the tortillas. Meanwhile, shred the turkey and toss together the lettuce and dressing.
5. Assemble the salads.
6. Garnish the gazpacho.

White Gazpacho

If you start with well-chilled vegetables—we usually refrigerate them overnight—the gazpacho, once prepared, will chill sufficiently in the time it takes you to make the salad. For the celery, choose a light green stalk from the center of the bunch. We've dispensed with the traditional soaking of bread in oil or water; it need only be moistened briefly.

10 ounces cucumber (about 1 cucumber)

5 ounces green bell pepper (about 1 small pepper)

1 ounce celery (about 1 small stalk)

2 cloves garlic

½ cup chopped white onion (precut)

2 slices light oatmeal bread

1¾ cups vegetable stock (see Pantry)

⅛ cup Tarragon White Wine Vinegar (see Pantry)

Salt to taste

2 tablespoons chopped fresh cilantro for garnish

Peel the cucumber, cut it in half lengthwise, and scrape out the seeds with the tip of a spoon. Cut each half crosswise into 4 pieces. Reserve 2 pieces for garnish. Trim the bell pepper and cut it into 8 chunks. Reserve 2 pieces for garnish. Cut the celery crosswise into 4 pieces. Peel the garlic.

In a food processor, combine the celery, onion, and all but the reserved pieces of cucumber and bell pepper. Press in the garlic.

Moisten the bread lightly with tap water, squeeze it dry, tear it into chunks, and add it to the mixture in the food processor. Add the vegetable stock and vinegar. Process for about 1 minute to a chunky puree. Season with salt.

Transfer to a bowl, cover, and refrigerate until ready to serve.

Chop the reserved cucumber and bell pepper for garnish.

Serve about ¾ cup soup in each of 4 bowls. Garnish with the chopped cilantro, cucumber, and bell pepper.

YIELD = 4 SERVINGS

Fat per serving = 0.37 g.

Calories per serving = 55.9

Turkey Caesar Salad

6 ounces turkey breast tenderloin

Two 7-inch corn tortillas

2 ounces roasted jalapeño peppers
(2 peppers, preroasted)

2 cloves garlic

½ cup skim milk ricotta cheese

¼ cup buttermilk

2 tablespoons freshly squeezed lime juice

¾ teaspoon anchovy paste

1 teaspoon Dijon mustard

Freshly ground black pepper to taste

One 10-ounce package cut romaine lettuce

1 teaspoon freshly grated Parmesan cheese

Preheat the broiler.

Broil the turkey for about 5 minutes per side, until lightly browned on the out-side and cooked through. Meanwhile, cut each tortilla into 12 wedges and place them in a single layer on a nonstick baking sheet. Core, seed, and cut the roasted peppers into strips (about 2 tablespoons plus 2 teaspoons). Peel the garlic. Remove the turkey and turn the oven down to 350 degrees.

For the dressing, combine the ricotta cheese, buttermilk, lime juice, anchovy paste, and mustard in a blender. Press in the garlic and add black pepper. Puree until smooth.

Bake the tortilla wedges for about 7 minutes, until lightly browned and crisp. Shred the turkey (about 1 cup). Combine the lettuce and dressing in a bowl and toss to coat thoroughly.

Divide the lettuce among 4 salad plates. Top each serving with about ¼ cup turkey, 2 teaspoons roasted peppers, and 6 tortilla wedges. Sprinkle each salad with ¼ teaspoon Parmesan cheese.

YIELD = 4 SERVINGS

Fat per serving = 0.98 g.

Calories per serving = 122.2

We love the convenience of preroasted jalapeño peppers, which can add a robust flavor accent to a range of dishes. However, unlike the sweet roasted variety, the jalapeños are packed in the jar whole and therefore must be cored and seeded.

Instead of using egg and oil for the Caesar dressing, we make a flavorful nonfat version using skim milk ricotta cheese and buttermilk. Butter-laden croutons are replaced with crisp, baked wedges of corn tortilla.

Crab and Okra Soup
Gnocchi with Blue Cheese Dressing

*A*lthough we usually make and serve the Creole-style soup first—with Buttermilk Biscuits (page 20) on the side—it's so filling one could argue that this was the main course. The soup derives its smoky flavor from liquid smoke rather than from the usual smoked ham hock. The equally rich, but not highly spiced gnocchi in cool blue cheese dressing is a perfect encore.

99% FAT-FREE FAST STRATEGY:

1. Prep the turkey and escarole for the soup.
2. Preheat a saucepan. Cook the onion in the hot pan, add the other soup ingredients, and boil.
3. Stir in the additional ingredients and simmer. Season and serve the soup.
4. Put a pot of water over high heat. While it comes to a boil, prep the roasted peppers and make the dressing for the gnocchi. Preheat a skillet.
5. Cook the gnocchi in the boiling water. Meanwhile, cook the vegetable mixture in the hot skillet.
6. Drain and add the gnocchi to the vegetable mixture. Remove from the heat and toss with the dressing.

Crab and Okra Soup

3¾ ounces sliced smoked turkey (about 4 thick slices)

14 ounces escarole (about 1 head)

Two 14½-ounce cans diced tomatoes with garlic and onion

One 6-ounce can lump crabmeat

½ cup chopped white onion (precut)

3½ cups vegetable stock (see Pantry)

1½ cups frozen sliced okra

1 tablespoon plus 1 teaspoon Old Bay seasoning

Freshly ground black pepper to taste

2 teaspoons liquid smoke

Cut the turkey into 1-× ¼-inch slices. Trim and roughly chop the escarole (about 4 cups). Drain the tomatoes and the crabmeat.

Preheat a large saucepan over high heat. Add the onion. Cook for 1 to 2 minutes, stirring constantly, until it begins to brown. Add the turkey, tomatoes, vegetable stock, okra, and Old Bay seasoning. Bring to a boil and boil for 3 minutes.

Stir in the escarole and crabmeat and bring back to a boil. Reduce the heat to medium and simmer for about 2 minutes, until the escarole has wilted completely. Add black pepper and stir in the liquid smoke.

Serve a generous 2 cups per person.

YIELD = 4 SERVINGS

Fat per serving = 0.86 g.

Calories per serving = 112.6

Liquid smoke, a natural hickory seasoning that comes bottled, can now be found in the spice section of many supermarkets.

Gnocchi with Blue Cheese Dressing

If you want to serve the gnocchi family style rather than plated, put the drained dumplings into a serving bowl, add the vegetable mixture, pour the dressing on top, and toss to coat.

6 ounces red chard (about 4 large leaves)

2 ounces sweet roasted peppers (preroasted)

1 pound potato gnocchi

¼ cup chopped white onion (precut)

2 tablespoons chopped fresh basil leaves

¼ cup Blue Cheese Dressing (page 32)

Trim and chop the chard (about 3 cups).

Bring a large pot of water to a boil over high heat. Meanwhile, rinse, drain, and dice the roasted peppers (about ¼ cup). Preheat a large nonstick skillet over high heat.

Put the gnocchi into the boiling water and cook for about 2 minutes, until the dumplings rise to the surface, then remove the pot from the heat.

Meanwhile, cook the onion in the hot skillet for about 2 minutes, until limp. Add the chard and roasted peppers. Cook for about 30 seconds, stirring constantly, until wilted. Drain and add the gnocchi. Stir in the basil, remove from the heat, and add the dressing. Toss and serve about 1 cup per person.

YIELD = 4 SERVINGS

Fat per serving = 0.99 g. (including dressing)

Calories per serving = 175.6 (including dressing)

Scallops and Spinach Gnocchi
Fennel and Artichoke Heart Salad

⌒

*T*his is one of our ultimate rush menus—it can be prepared from start to finish in about fifteen minutes, bringing water to boil being the single most time-consuming step! The combination of the green spinach gnocchi, the white scallops, and the red of the tomatoes in the sauce makes for a very colorful plate. The pairing of lime juice and tequila with scallops is a take on classic seviche, only lightly cooked.

Serve the salad alongside the main course. The crunch of the raw fennel and snap peas provides an interesting contrast to the tender texture of the scallops and gnocchi, while the taste of the fennel plays nicely off the tequila in the sauce.

99% FAT-FREE FAST STRATEGY:

1. Put a large pot of water over high heat.
2. While it comes to a boil, make the garlic dressing, combine the salad ingredients, and dress and season the salad. Preheat a skillet.
3. Cook the gnocchi in the boiling water. Meanwhile, cook the sauce in the hot skillet.
4. Drain and toss the gnocchi in the sauce.
5. Plate the salad atop the lettuce leaves.

Scallops and Spinach Gnocchi

This recipe can easily be cut in half to feed 2. Stored in the freezer, leftover uncooked gnocchi will keep for up to a month. It can easily be retrieved by handfuls and thrown into boiling water; serve it with any good, low-fat tomato sauce for an eminently satisfying last-minute dinner.

One 14½-ounce can stewed tomatoes

1 pound spinach gnocchi

1 teaspoon minced roasted garlic (precut)

12 ounces bay scallops

2 tablespoons snipped fresh chives

1 tablespoon packed sliced fresh basil leaves

3 tablespoons freshly squeezed lime juice

1 tablespoon tequila

Bring a large pot of water to a boil over high heat. Preheat a medium nonstick skillet over medium-high heat. Drain the tomatoes.

Add the gnocchi to the boiling water and cook for 2 to 2½ minutes, until the dumplings rise to the top of the pot.

Meanwhile, add the tomatoes and garlic to the hot skillet and cook for 30 seconds, stirring constantly and breaking up the larger pieces of tomato with a spoon. Add the scallops and cook for about 30 seconds, stirring, until they are just beginning to turn opaque. Raise the heat to high and add the chives, basil, lime juice, and tequila. Cook and stir for 30 to 45 seconds more, until the scallops are completely opaque. Drain the gnocchi and toss it with the mixture in the skillet.

Serve about ¾ cup per person.

YIELD = 4 SERVINGS

Fat per serving = 0.87 g.

Calories per serving = 222.0

Fennel and Artichoke Heart Salad

8 ounces fennel

4 ounces fresh sugar snap peas (about 1 cup)

One 9-ounce package frozen artichoke hearts, thawed

½ tablespoon sliced fresh basil leaves

¼ cup Garlic Spread (page 148)

Salt and freshly ground black pepper to taste

4 leaves red-leaf lettuce

Trim and cut the fennel in half lengthwise, then slice it crosswise into thin wedges (about 1½ cups).

In a bowl, combine the fennel, sugar snap peas, and artichoke hearts. Add the basil and stir to mix.

Add the garlic spread to the bowl and toss to coat. Season with salt and pepper. Line each of 4 salad plates with a lettuce leaf. Divide the salad among the plates.

YIELD = 4 SERVINGS

Fat per serving = 0.37 g. (including dressing)
Calories per serving = 63.7 (including dressing)

Pasta with Fresh Clam Sauce
Eggplant Steaks

—

*I*n this light but satisfying meal, the eggplant steaks serve as a warm salad to accompany the wonderfully fresh seafood pasta. We cook the clams in their shells in a hot pan—the same pan in which the pasta sauce will be prepared, saving the bother of another dirty pot and eliminating the more cumbersome task of shucking the clams raw. Essentially steaming, this method of cooking allows the clams to open slowly and leaves them sweet, juicy, and tender.

We usually pass freshly grated Parmesan cheese at the table for those who wish to indulge.

99% FAT-FREE FAST STRATEGY:
1. Rinse the clams while preheating a skillet.
2. Cook the clams in the hot skillet, shaking the pan periodically.
3. While the clams cook, prep and salt the eggplant and prep the roasted pepper.
4. Put a pot of water over high heat. While it comes to a boil, shuck and slice the clams. Preheat the broiler.
5. Cook the pasta in the boiling water. Meanwhile, cook the red pepper topping for the eggplant.
6. Rinse, dry, and precook the eggplant in a microwave. Preheat the skillet once more.
7. While broiling the eggplant, cook the pasta sauce in the hot skillet.
8. Toss the pasta in the sauce and top the eggplant steaks with the pepper mixture.

Pasta with Fresh Clam Sauce

1¼ pounds littleneck clams (about 16 clams)

One 14½-ounce can diced tomatoes with basil, oregano, and garlic

6 ounces fideos (thin Spanish or Mexican pasta)

1 teaspoon minced garlic (precut)

¾ cup bottled clam juice

Pinch of crushed red pepper

2 tablespoons chopped fresh flat-leaf parsley

Put the clams in a colander and shake them under cold running water for about 1 minute. Discard any clams that do not close when tapped. Drain the tomatoes.

Preheat a large nonstick skillet over high heat.

Transfer the clams to the hot skillet, cover, and reduce the heat to medium-high. Cook for 1 minute, shaking the pan periodically. Uncover the pan and reduce the heat to medium. Cook for about 10 minutes, shaking the pan often and flipping the clams over, until they have opened slightly and can be pried opened easily.

Shuck the clams and cut each one into 2 to 3 pieces. Transfer the clams and any residual juice to a bowl, cover, and set aside. Meanwhile, bring a large pot of water to a boil over high heat. Add the pasta to the boiling water. Reduce the heat to medium-high and cook until al dente, about 6 minutes. Drain. Meanwhile, preheat the skillet once more, this time over medium heat.

Combine the tomatoes and garlic in the hot skillet. Cook for about 15 seconds, stirring, until the liquid has evaporated. Add the clam juice and crushed red pepper. Cook for about 1 minute, stirring, until the mixture is steaming. Add the pasta and toss. Cook and toss for about 1 minute more, until the liquid has been absorbed. Add the parsley and clams and toss over the heat to warm. Serve about 1 cup per person.

YIELD = 4 SERVINGS

Fat per serving = 0.52 g.

Calories per serving = 167.6

If you substitute the same weight of larger cherrystone clams for the littlenecks, cut them into eighths after cooking. Don't be alarmed if the shells leave a bit of white residue on the surface of the nonstick pan while cooking; it should wash right off. If you prefer, use an uncoated pan to cook the clams and then spray the pan lightly with vegetable oil cooking spray before proceeding, or switch to a nonstick pan for the sauce.

Eggplant Steaks

Salting tends to take the slightly bitter edge off eggplant and accentuate its underlying sweetness. In warm weather we often pair this dish with Yellow Chowder (page 147) and a basket of Buttermilk Biscuits (page 20).

1 pound purple eggplant (about 1 small eggplant)

½ teaspoon coarse kosher salt

6 ounces sweet roasted peppers (preroasted)

½ cup chopped white onion (precut)

1 teaspoon minced garlic (precut)

¾ teaspoon dried oregano

¼ cup dry white wine

Salt and freshly ground black pepper to taste

Trim the eggplant and cut a thin slice off each side to flatten and expose the meat under the skin. Cut lengthwise into 4 slices about ¾ inch thick. Sprinkle the steaks liberally with kosher salt and place them in a colander to drain.

Preheat the broiler. Line a broiler pan with aluminum foil.

Rinse, drain, and chop the roasted peppers (about ⅔ cup). In a small saucepan, combine the roasted peppers, onion, garlic, oregano, and wine. Cover and cook over medium heat for 7 to 8 minutes, until the onion is soft and translucent. Remove from the heat and set aside, covered.

Rinse the eggplant under cold running water, pat dry, and put on a plate in a single layer. Cover loosely with plastic wrap and microwave at full power for about 3 minutes, until soft and steaming. Transfer to the prepared broiler tray and cook for about 2 minutes per side, until browned.

Remove each steak to a salad plate. Top with about ¼ cup of the roasted pepper mixture and season with salt and pepper.

YIELD = 4 SERVINGS

Fat per serving = 0.21 g.

Calories per serving = 53.4

Cream of Cauliflower Soup
Mahimahi Burgers
Coleslaw

—

A somewhat healthier and more sophisticated update of classic summer-time burgers and slaw, this menu can be whipped up in about 20 minutes, and it works equally well as luncheon fare or as a casual dinner. The recipes encompass an interesting complexity of flavors, ranging from the sweet hoisin sauce in the burgers—juxtaposed if desired with fiery wasabi, a grated Japanese horseradish traditionally served with sushi—to the gingery flavor of the coleslaw and the hint of cumin in the soup.

99% FAT-FREE FAST STRATEGY:

1. Start the soup. While it simmers, preheat the broiler. Crumb the bread, grind the fish, and make the burgers.
2. Puree the soup. Return it to the pan, finish cooking, and keep warm over low heat.
3. While broiling the burgers, make the dressing and mix the slaw.
4. Garnish the soup.

Cream of Cauliflower Soup

6 cups cauliflower florets (precut)

3/4 cup chopped white onion (precut)

3 cups water

1 teaspoon salt

1/2 cup evaporated skim milk

1/2 teaspoon ground cumin

1/8 teaspoon ground white pepper

Snipped fresh chives for garnish

In a large saucepan, combine the cauliflower, onion, water, and salt. Bring to a boil over high heat. Cover, reduce the heat to medium-low, and simmer for 10 to 12 minutes, until the vegetables are soft enough to be mashed easily.

Transfer the contents of the pan to a food processor or blender and puree.

Return the puree to the saucepan over medium-low heat. Stir in the evaporated milk, cumin, and white pepper. Heat for about 1 minute. Keep warm over low heat until ready to serve (do not allow it to come to a boil).

Ladle 1 cup into each of 6 soup bowls and garnish with the chives.

YIELD = 6 SERVINGS

Fat per serving = 0.22 g.

Calories per serving = 39.9

Mahimahi Burgers

2 slices light oatmeal bread

1 pound mahimahi

1 pound Pacific cod

¼ cup Chinese hoisin sauce

2 teaspoons wasabi powder (optional)

Preheat the broiler. Line a broiler tray with aluminum foil.

Put the bread in a food processor and process to crumbs (about ½ cup). Transfer it to a mixing bowl.

Combine the mahimahi and cod in the food processor and process until ground. Add the fish to the mixing bowl with the crumbs. Add the hoisin sauce and wasabi powder, if desired. Mix well and form into 6 patties.

Place the patties on the prepared tray and broil for about 3 minutes per side, until browned on the outside and no longer pink inside.

YIELD = 6 SERVINGS

Fat per serving = 0.93 g.

Calories per serving = 171.2

These meatless burgers will satisfy even the most dedicated carnivores. The inclusion of extremely low-fat cod produces a tasty burger with less fat than would result from using mahimahi alone; be sure to buy Pacific cod, which is much lower in fat than any other variety.

Coleslaw

4 cups shredded green cabbage (precut)

2 cups shredded carrots (precut)

2 tablespoons grated ginger (precut)

¼ cup plus 2 tablespoons white wine
vinegar

1 tablespoon plus 1 teaspoon Dijon
mustard

½ cup light corn syrup

In a mixing bowl, combine the cabbage and carrots.

In another bowl, combine the ginger, vinegar, and mustard. Whisk in the corn syrup. Pour the dressing over the cabbage and carrot mixture and toss to coat.

Serve about 1 cup per person.

YIELD = 6 SERVINGS

Fat per serving = 0.44 g.

Calories per serving = 75.4

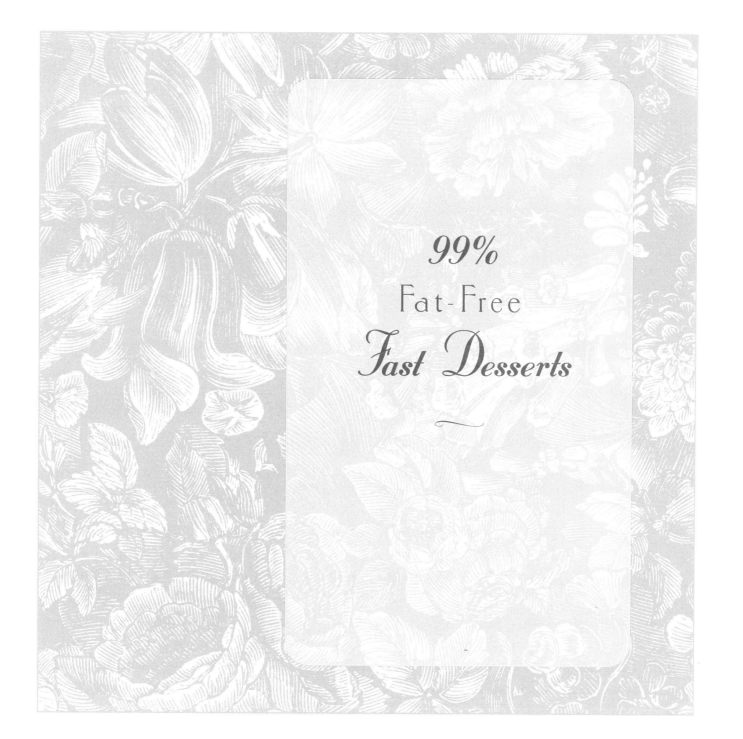

99%
Fat-Free
Fast Desserts

Carrot Soufflé with Carrot Sauce

This quick yet spectacular dessert makes a fitting end to such holiday feasts as our Thanksgiving dinner (page 130). The recipe can be prepared through the initial heating of the carrot mixture before you sit down at the table. For the best results, beat the egg whites in a heavy stationary mixer.

Vegetable oil cooking spray

2 tablespoons granulated sugar

6 ounces frozen organic carrot baby food

2 teaspoons minced crystallized ginger

1 teaspoon ground cinnamon

¾ teaspoon pumpkin pie spice

½ tablespoon all-purpose flour

1 tablespoon Triple Sec liqueur

¼ cup packed dark brown sugar

4 large egg whites, at room temperature

Confectioners' sugar for dusting

CARROT SAUCE:

2 ounces frozen organic carrot baby food, thawed

2 tablespoons Triple Sec liqueur

1 teaspoon freshly grated orange zest

Preheat the oven to 375 degrees.

Spray a 1-quart soufflé dish or a straight-sided casserole once with vegetable oil cooking spray and smooth the oil evenly over the surface. Sprinkle 1 tablespoon of the granulated sugar lightly over the dish to coat the entire inside surface.

In a small saucepan, combine the carrot, crystallized ginger, cinnamon, pumpkin pie spice, flour, Triple Sec, and brown sugar. Cook over low heat for 1 to 2 minutes, stirring constantly with a wooden spoon, just until the mixture begins to steam. Remove it to a large mixing bowl and set aside.

Beat the egg whites to soft peaks with an electric mixer at low speed. Add the remaining tablespoon of granulated sugar and continue to beat until soft, moist peaks form. Add a third of the egg whites to the carrot mixture and whisk to incorporate thoroughly. Gently fold in the remaining egg whites until evenly distributed.

Pour into the prepared soufflé dish or casserole. With your fingers, make a ½- to ¾-inch deep ridge around the inside rim. Bake for 18 to 20 minutes, until the top of the soufflé has puffed up and browned.

Meanwhile, make the sauce: In a bowl, combine all the ingredients and whisk to mix thoroughly.

Dust the soufflé with confectioners' sugar. Scoop it out with a large spoon, dividing it among 4 dessert plates. Spoon 1 tablespoon plus 1 teaspoon of the sauce alongside each serving.

YIELD = 4 SERVINGS

Fat per serving = 0.20 g.

Calories per serving = 201.7

Humongous Chocolate Brownies with Chocolate Frosting

Since these oversize delights are well within our fat range, we're throwing caution to the wind and indulging in a few extra calories; if you're counting calories, know that half a serving would still be a generous portion.

This should finally lay to rest the doubts of any remaining skeptics who say you can't make a scrumptious low-fat brownie. It's our third, following in the footsteps of The 99% Fat-Free Cookbook's Old-Fashioned Cocoa Brownies and The 99% Fat-Free Book of Appetizers and Desserts's Fudgy Raspberry Brownies.

3/4 cup Dutch (European style) processed cocoa powder

1/2 cup plus 2 tablespoons boiling water

1/4 cup light corn syrup

1 teaspoon instant coffee granules (optional)

3/4 cup nonfat liquid egg substitute

1 1/2 cups granulated sugar

2/3 cup natural unsweetened applesauce

3/4 cup all-purpose flour

CHOCOLATE FROSTING:

1 cup confectioners' sugar

2 tablespoons Dutch (European style) processed cocoa powder

3 tablespoons water

Preheat the oven to 350 degrees.

In a small bowl, combine the cocoa powder, boiling water, corn syrup, and, if desired for a slightly richer-tasting brownie, the instant coffee granules. Mix with a wooden spoon or a spatula until smooth and glossy.

Put the egg substitute into a large mixing bowl and whisk a few times until frothy. Add the granulated sugar and whisk until combined, slightly thickened, and pale, about 30 seconds. Whisk in the applesauce, then the cocoa mixture. Mix in the flour with a wooden spoon.

Pour the batter into a 9-inch nonstick pan. Bake for about 20 minutes, until firm. Cool in the pan on a wire rack.

Meanwhile, make the frosting. Combine all the ingredients in a bowl and mix thoroughly with a rubber spatula until smooth. Spread over the brownies to cover. Cut into 3-inch squares.

YIELD = 9 BROWNIES

Fat per serving = 0.86 g.
Calories per brownie = 287.3

Chocolate Fondue

Serve this rich, not-too-sweet chocolate sauce in a fondue pot over a medium flame, alongside an arrangement of fresh fruit. Use fondue forks or 12-inch bamboo skewers for dipping. By itself, the sauce can be used to top sorbets, sherbets, or frozen yogurt.

One 4-ounce blood orange

1 pint strawberries

8 ounces peach (about 1 peach)

6 ounces banana (about 1 banana)

1 teaspoon freshly squeezed lemon juice

CHOCOLATE SAUCE:

1/4 cup plus 2 tablespoons unsweetened
   Dutch processed cocoa powder

2/3 cup sugar

2 tablespoons light corn syrup

1/4 cup skim milk

1/2 teaspoon vanilla extract

1 teaspoon Grand Marnier liqueur
   (optional)

Peel and separate the blood orange into sections. Hull the strawberries. Stone and cut the peach into 12 wedges. Peel and cut the banana on the diagonal into 12 slices; sprinkle with the lemon juice.

For the sauce: In a small nonstick saucepan, combine the cocoa powder, sugar, corn syrup, and milk. Cook over medium heat for 6 to 7 minutes, stirring frequently, until the mixture is smooth and glossy. Remove from the heat and stir in the vanilla and, if desired, the liqueur.

YIELD = 1 CUP CHOCOLATE SAUCE, OR 6 SERVINGS

Fat per serving = 0.91 g. (including fruit)

Calories per serving = 208.9 (including fruit)

Bananas Foster

1 pound bananas (about 2 bananas)   1 tablespoon light rum
1 tablespoon dark brown sugar

Preheat the broiler. Line a shallow baking dish with aluminum foil.

Peel the bananas and cut each one in half lengthwise, then crosswise. Lay the quarters flat side up in the prepared dish.

Mix the brown sugar and rum and pour the mixture evenly over the bananas. Broil for about 2 minutes, until bubbly and browned. Serve 2 quarters on each of 4 dessert plates alongside a topping of your choice, if desired. Drizzle with residual syrup from the broiling dish.

YIELD = 4 SERVINGS

Fat per serving = 0.30 g.

Calories per serving = 73.3

A full-flavored classic pared of superfluous fat, this dish is wonderful topped with Piña Colada Sherbet (page 187) or Creamy Whipped Topping made with rum (see Pantry).

Individual Raspberry Gratins

Your guests will think you slaved over these elegant little gratins enclosed in a silky crème anglaise–style custard.

1 pint raspberries

1 cup evaporated skim milk

3 tablespoons nonfat liquid egg substitute

2 tablespoons confectioners' sugar

½ tablespoon framboise liqueur

Preheat the oven to 400 degrees.

Place ½ cup of the raspberries in a single layer on the bottom of each of 4 individual gratin dishes, small scalloped shells, or other shallow, ovenproof dishes.

Combine the remaining ingredients in a mixing bowl and whisk until the sugar has dissolved completely. Pour over the raspberries.

Place the dishes on a baking or cookie sheet and bake for about 15 minutes, until thick and bubbly. Serve immediately.

YIELD = 4 SERVINGS

Fat per serving = 0.55 g.

Calories per serving = 110.7

Blueberry and Peach Shortcakes

6 ounces peach (about 1 peach)

½ pint blueberries

2 tablespoons sugar

2 tablespoons Grand Marnier liqueur

4 Buttermilk Biscuits (see Pantry)

½ cup Creamy Whipped Topping made
 with Grand Marnier (see Pantry)

Stone and chop the peach (about 1 cup). Pick over the blueberries.

Combine the fruit in a mixing bowl. Add the sugar and liqueur and mix.

Split the biscuits open and mound the bottom half of each one with about ½ cup of the fruit mixture. Top each with 2 tablespoons of the whipped topping and serve with the other biscuit half on the side.

YIELD = 4 SERVINGS

Fat per serving = 0.97 g.

Calories per serving = 276.3

This treat was inspired by the Individual Strawberry Shortcakes in our 99% Fat-Free Book of Appetizers and Desserts.

Plum Gratin

In this gratin, we encase fresh plums in thick custard with a brown sugar topping, rather like a crème brûlée.

8 ounces purple plums (about 2 plums)

¾ cup evaporated skim milk

¼ cup nonfat liquid egg substitute

2 tablespoons confectioners' sugar

½ tablespoon brandy

¾ teaspoon freshly grated nutmeg

2 tablespoons packed dark brown sugar

Preheat the broiler.

Stone the plums and cut each one into 16 wedges. Place 8 wedges into each of 4 individual gratin dishes in a single layer.

In a bowl, combine the evaporated milk, egg substitute, confectioners' sugar, brandy, and nutmeg and whisk to dissolve the sugar thoroughly. Pour over the plums. Scatter ½ tablespoon of the brown sugar over each gratin.

Broil for 2 to 3 minutes, until the gratins are lightly browned and bubbly.

YIELD = 4 SERVINGS

Fat per serving = 0.55 g.

Calories per serving = 118.8

Coffee Gelatin

2 tablespoons Kahlúa liqueur

¼ ounce (1 envelope) unflavored gelatin

1½ cups warm brewed coffee

1 tablespoon sugar

2 ice cubes

½ cup Creamy Whipped Topping made
with Kahlúa liqueur (see Pantry)

Put the liqueur into a bowl and sprinkle it with the gelatin. Let stand for 2 minutes to soften. Add the coffee and sugar. Stir until the gelatin and sugar have dissolved. Add the ice cubes and stir until they have melted. Pour the mixture into an 8-inch square pan and freeze it for about 30 minutes, until gelled.

Cut the gelatin into ¾-inch cubes and put ½ cup into each of 4 wineglasses. Refrigerate until ready to serve. Top each serving with 2 tablespoons of the whipped topping.

YIELD = 4 SERVINGS

Fat per serving = 0.06 g.

Calories per serving = 89.8

Make this unique, light dessert a bit ahead of time and let it chill and harden in the freezer while you prepare and eat your dinner.

Pear-Ginger Sorbet

It doesn't get much easier than making luscious sorbets and sherbets from frozen canned fruit. Gratification is almost instantaneous—you don't even need to wait for an ice cream maker to do its thing. This sorbet features our favorite flavor combination, pears and ginger.

One 15¼-ounce can pear halves in heavy syrup, frozen

1 tablespoon grated ginger (precut)

2 tablespoons vodka

Put the can of pears in a bowl and place it under hot running water for about 30 seconds. Remove the contents of the can to a cutting board and cut into thirds crosswise, then quarter each piece.

Transfer the pears to a food processor. Wrap the ginger in paper toweling and squeeze the juice into the food processor. Pulse 20 times. Turn the machine on, add the vodka, and process for 30 seconds. Scrape down the sides of the food processor with a rubber spatula, stir, and process for about 15 seconds more, until the mixture is almost smooth. Serve at once.

YIELD = 2 CUPS, OR 4 SERVINGS

Fat per serving = 0.11 g.

Calories per serving = 97.4

Cherry Sorbet

One 17-ounce can pitted Royal Anne
    cherries in extra-heavy syrup,
    frozen

¼ teaspoon pure almond extract

2 tablespoons brandy

Put the can of cherries in a bowl and place it under hot running water for about 30 seconds. Remove the contents of the can to a cutting board and cut into quarters, then transfer to a food processor.

Add the almond extract and pulse 20 times. Turn the machine on, add the brandy, and process for 10 to 12 seconds, until smooth. Serve at once.

YIELD = 2 CUPS, OR 4 SERVINGS

Fat per serving = 0.21 g.

Calories per serving = 117.0

Cherry sorbet makes a refreshing finish for a light summertime meal. When making sorbets and sherbets using canned fruit, freeze the fruit in the can for at least 8 hours.

Mandarin Orange Sherbet

This cool and creamy frozen dessert is a perfect way to end a spicy meal. The easiest way to remove frozen fruit from the can is to take off both the top and bottom lids and push the fruit out.

Two 11-ounce cans Mandarin oranges in light syrup, frozen

¼ cup evaporated skim milk

Put the cans of oranges in a bowl under hot running water for about 30 seconds. Remove the contents of the cans to a cutting board, quarter, and transfer to a food processor. Pulse 20 times. Turn the machine on, add the evaporated milk, and process for 1 to 2 minutes, until smooth. Serve immediately.

YIELD = 3 CUPS, OR 6 SERVINGS

Fat per serving = 0.02 g.

Calories per serving = 73.0

Piña Colada Sherbet

Two 8¼-ounce cans crushed pineapple in heavy syrup, frozen

1 tablespoon light rum
1½ tablespoons light coconut milk

Open the tops and bottoms of the cans and cut each block of frozen pineapple into quarters. Push the contents out of the cans into a food processor. Add the rum and pulse 10 times. Turn the machine on, drizzle in the coconut milk, and process for about 30 seconds, until smooth. Serve at once.

YIELD = 2 CUPS, OR 4 SERVINGS

Fat per serving = 0.38 g.

Calories per serving = 103.5

Cut frozen fruit for sherbets and sorbets into segments with a large, sturdy knife.

Blueberry Sorbet

One 15-ounce can wild Maine
    blueberries in heavy syrup, frozen

2 tablespoons Triple Sec liqueur

Put the can of blueberries in a bowl under hot running water for 20 seconds. Remove the contents of the can to a cutting board and cut into 6 chunks. Transfer to a food processor and pulse 5 times. Turn the machine on and process for 5 seconds while drizzling in the liqueur. Stir and process for about 10 seconds more, until smooth. Serve immediately.

YIELD = 2 CUPS, OR 4 SERVINGS

Fat per serving = 0.27 g.

Calories per serving = 86.0

When transferring frozen fruit for sorbets and sherbets from the cutting board to the food processor, be sure to also transfer any residual juices that have accumulated on the board.

Apricot Sorbet

One 17-ounce can apricot halves in heavy
 syrup, frozen

¼ teaspoon orange extract

1 teaspoon freshly grated orange zest

2 tablespoons apricot brandy

For a special treat, drizzle
the sorbet with Chocolate
Fondue sauce (page 178).

Put the can of apricots in a bowl under hot running water for about 45 seconds. Remove the contents of the can to a cutting board and cut into 8 chunks. Transfer to a
food processor. Add the orange extract and zest and pulse 15 times. Turn the machine
on and add the brandy. Process for 30 seconds, stir, and process for about 15 seconds
more, until smooth. Serve at once.

YIELD = 2 CUPS, OR 4 SERVINGS

Fat per serving = 0.11 g.

Calories per serving = 117.3

Strawberry Sorbet

If desired, garnish the sorbet with fresh blueberries for a striking color contrast.

Two 10-ounce packages frozen strawberries

2 tablespoons freshly squeezed orange juice

1 teaspoon finely grated fresh orange zest

Combine all the ingredients in a food processor. Process for 10 seconds. Stir to mix and process for about 5 seconds more, until almost smooth. Serve at once.

YIELD = 2½ CUPS, OR 5 SERVINGS

Fat per serving = 0.17 g.

Calories per serving = 92.0

Fig Sorbet

One 17-ounce can whole split Kadota figs 2 tablespoons tawny port
 in heavy syrup, frozen

Put the can of figs in a bowl and place under hot running water for about 20 seconds.

Open the can and pour any liquid into a food processor.

Push the solid contents out onto a cutting board and cut the block into 8 pieces. Transfer to the food processor and pulse 25 to 30 times, until smooth, while drizzling in the port. Return the sorbet to the freezer for about 30 minutes, or until you are ready to serve.

YIELD = 2 CUPS, OR 4 SERVINGS

Fat per serving = 0.11 g.

Calories per serving = 122.3

For the best consistency, make this sorbet before dinner and let it harden a bit in the freezer while you eat.

Appendix: Recipes by Course

PASTA, GRAIN, AND VEGETABLE-BASED ENTRÉES

Broccoli, Shiitake, and Chicken Stir-Fry (page 101)

Gnocchi Lumache (page 55)

Gnocchi with Blue Cheese Dressing (page 162)

Lasagna (page 95)

Mediterranean Pasta (page 103)

Mexican Lasagna (page 106)

Michael Silverstein's Penne with Asparagus and Smoked Turkey (page 46)

Moroccan Vegetables and Chicken (page 62)

Pad Thai (page 112)

Pasta with Fresh Clam Sauce (page 167)

Portobello Stir-Fry (page 67)

Potato and Pepper Frittata (page 57)

Shrimp, Leek, and Asparagus Risotto (page 43)

Vegetable and Seafood Paella (page 35)

SIDE DISHES

Asparagus in Black Bean Sauce (page 85)

Chinese Rice (page 99)

Chive Noodles (page 117)

Citrus Salsa (page 151)

Corn Muffins (page 123)

Cumin Basmati Rice (page 87)

Cumin Couscous (page 63)

Curried Rice (page 155)

Garlic Noodle Sauté (page 81)

Mushroom Orzo (page 66)

Potato-Fennel Gratin (page 131)

Refried Black Beans (page 152)

Roasted Garlic Potatoes (page 28)

Sautéed Chard (page 145)

Scallion Noodles (page 129)

Sweet and Sour Cabbage (page 116)

Tomato Bread (page 97)

Wilted Zucchini (page 27)

DESSERTS

Apricot Sorbet (page 189)

Bananas Foster (page 179)

Blueberry and Peach Shortcakes (page 181)

Blueberry Sorbet (page 188)

Carrot Soufflé with Carrot Sauce (page 174)

Cherry Sorbet (page 185)

Chocolate Fondue (page 178)

Coffee Gelatin (page 183)